Canadian Confederation:
A Decision-Making Analysis

W. L. WHITE,
R. H. WAGENBERG,
R. C. NELSON,
W. C. SODERLUND

THE CARLETON LIBRARY NO. 117
Published by Macmillan of Canada
in association with the Institute of
Canadian Studies, Carleton University

BRESCIA COLLEGE
LIBRARY

45887

COPYRIGHT © W. L. White, R. H. Wagenberg,
R. C. Nelson and W. C. Soderlund 1979

All rights reserved—no part of this book may
be reproduced in any form without
permission in writing from the publisher
except by a reviewer who wishes to quote
brief passages in connection with a review
written for inclusion in a magazine or
newspaper.

Canadian Cataloguing in Publication Data

Main entry under title:

Canadian Confederation

(The Carleton library; no. 117)

Bibliography: p.
ISBN 0-7705-1795-1 pa.

1. Canada—History—Confederation, 1967.*
2. Canada—Politics and government—1841-
1867.
I. White, Walter L., 1921-1975.   II. Carleton
University. Institute of Canadian Studies.
III. Series.

FC474.C35   971.04'9   C79-094354-9
F1032.C35

Printed in Canada for
The Macmillan Company of Canada Limited
70 Bond Street
Toronto, Ontario
M5B 1X3

The Carleton Library

A series of reprints, original works, and new
collections of source material relating to
Canada, issued under the editorial
supervision of the Institute of Canadian
Studies of Carleton University, Ottawa.

Director of the Institute
S. F. Wise

General Editor
Michael Gnarowski

Executive Editor
Virgil D. Duff (*Macmillan of Canada*)

Editorial Board
Marilyn J. Barber (*History*)
Dennis Forcese (*Sociology*)
David B. Knight (*Geography*)
Steven Langdon (*Economics*)
Maureen Molot (*Political Science*)
J. George Neuspiel (*Law*)
Derek G. Smith (*Anthropology*)

Publications Editor
James H. Marsh

FOR WALTER;
*friend, colleague, teacher and
extraordinary human being.*

Contents

List of Figures and Tables

Preface

Walter White had a deep interest in the problems of Canadian federalism. After a long period of reflection on the kind of research that
needed to be done on this subject, he began preliminary work on this
project in January 1973. He interested the rest of us in joining him
over the following spring and summer. After working on the project
for over two years, Walter died suddenly on February 3, 1975.

In addition to providing the initial idea for the book and directing
the project, Walter participated in every phase of the research, which
was over half completed at the time of his death. He also wrote the
first draft of the introductory chapter and left notes and working
drafts, parts of which we have incorporated into chapters 2, 3, and 7.
The final manuscript unquestionably would have benefited from his
further guidance and participation.

We are grateful for the inspiration and enthusiasm which Walter
conveyed to all who knew him. It made the years following his
untimely death somewhat less empty and gave us a sense of dedica-
tion to see the project through to its completion. A scholarship was
established at the University of Windsor in memory of Walter, and
we feel it fitting that whatever royalties accrue through the sale of this
book should be placed in that scholarship fund.

We would like to express our thanks to a number of people who
helped in getting this book written and published. Special mention
goes to Michael Whittington, the Carleton Library Series Political
Science Editor, James Marsh, the Carleton Library Series Publications
Editor, and Virgil Duff of Macmillan of Canada. Kenneth Pryke of
the Department of History at the University of Windsor was always
most helpful in answering questions. Finally, we would like to convey
our gratitude to our wives and children for their patience, and especially to Walter's wife Juel, who typed the many drafts involved in
producing the final manuscript.

Windsor, Ontario

R. H. Wagenberg
R. C. Nelson
W. C. Soderlund

CHAPTER ONE

Introduction

One hundred and thirteen years after the debates in the Parliament of the Province of Canada regarding Confederation, the question of the basic constitutional structure of the country is again a main pre-occupation of political leaders and citizens alike. The increased demands on the part of western provinces, particularly, for greater control over their resources through self-regulation of pricing or nationalization, has been no doubt overshadowed by the election in 1976 of the Parti Québécois, which is committed to the separation of Quebec from Confederation. Both, however, are indicators that the Canadian federal system is going through a centrifugal phase of so radical a nature as to threaten the constitutional structure itself.

Throughout the historical development of Canadian federalism power has at times centred in Ottawa, with tendencies toward a unitary system; at other times the locus of power has shifted towards the provinces. A swing from centralism to devolution is best seen in a relatively short period of time during which the Manitoba School question of the 1890s was being considered. Initially, there were strong pressures on the central government, at that time in the hands of the Conservative Party, to intervene under the provisions of the BNA Act, Section 93, and overturn the provincial legislation which had denied state support to Catholic Schools. The Conservative government, in line with its centralist position, which had been established under Macdonald and had been maintained during the early years of Confederation, agreed that remedial legislation would be introduced. However, the 1896 election brought a change in government, and the Liberal prime minister, Wilfrid Laurier, refused to proceed with remedial legislation. This refusal ushered in an era during which the central government's powers to intervene in the affairs of the provinces, under the provisions of the BNA Act, were used with less and less frequency, and ultimately their use has ceased entirely. Such shifts of power are not accidental to federal systems but constitute rather the federal dynamic. If federalism is essentially

1

the politics of accommodation, it is also by that fact the most flexible kind of political system, and it is far from evident that "co-operative federalism"[1] is the last word concerning the relations between the federal government and the provinces. Perhaps we are now seeing the termination of a long period in which the powers of the federal government have been increased to the detriment of the provinces.[2] In other words, we are not convinced from an examination of the development of Canadian federalism that the alternatives for the system articulated by spokesmen for national unity on one side and separatism on the other exhaust the practicable options. Have we not seen the system develop in ways undreamed of by its founders, who were themselves reluctant federalists at best? And given the modalities of the federal-provincial relationship over a period of more than a century, there is room to hope that this latest crisis may not have the dire consequences which were initially feared.

At any specific time, political imagination seems to operate within narrow limitations. One can think, for instance, of the alternative between monarchism and republicanism which dominated so much of eighteenth century political discourse, or the alternative between liberal and autocratic states which preoccupied European policy makers in the first half of the nineteenth century. In the same vein, the great wave of nationalist ideology in Europe has endured despite the appeals of proletarian internationalism or the politics of the "good European", that is, one who seeks an integrated federal Europe.

In order for contemporary statesmen to understand the range of alternatives within a federal political system, it seems to us that two kinds of academic study are important. One focuses on comparative federalism, where in recent years a literature dealing with non-American forms of federalism has produced significant alternative perspectives on the ways in which federal systems can operate.[3] The second, and that which we intend to pursue, is a genetic approach, which seeks to understand the system in terms of the circumstances of its generation, or origin.

In this sense, Confederation is among the most important events in Canada's political history. From Confederation stemmed the development of the Canadian Parliamentary system in a federal structure, for Confederation set the parameters in which the political system developed. The major aspects of the debate over Confederation which we shall examine—culture, politics, economics, and external relations—all find their resolution in the construction of a federal political system. Moreover, all the institutions and vital elements of the political process, such as political parties and pressure groups, as well as the various arenas of politics, grew and responded to an environment largely set by the decision made in the mid-1860s to create a dual ethnic, multi-regional federal state.

While the importance of Confederation is often implicitly assumed, most of the scholarly interpretations directed at the omnibus character of Confederation and federalism in Canada have not analysed closely the Confederation event as the point of origin of the Canadian federal system. There is, therefore, an *a priori* character to the major part of the writing on Canadian federalism by political scientists: an assumption that perhaps it can be best studied by looking at the complex political effects of federalism since 1867. This approach to federalism has focused largely on the structure and process of the system, with some concentration on the adaptability of the system to a changing political environment.

The importance of understanding the effects of the environment on the political system has been pointed out by Alan C. Cairns in a recent review article.

> The Canadian political system, like any other, is a result of previous political decisions, historical events, antecedent social forces, etc. It cannot be understood without resort to history.[4]

While it is difficult to argue with Cairns' position, the problem with his observation is that it is so general that it provides few concrete guidelines for determining what is important in a country's historical experience.

In this regard, our own research focus has been heavily influenced by two key works, Barrington Moore Jr.'s *Social Origins of Dictatorship and Democracy*[5], and Louis Hartz' *The Founding of New Societies*.[6] While these two important books differ in many ways, Moore finding the determinants to the subsequent development of dictatorial or democratic regimes in the pattern of the breakup of the feudal system, and Hartz pointing to the character of European immigration as the decisive variable explaining the future development of the state, both share the common theoretical notion that the point of origin of a system is of decisive importance in understanding the development of that system.[7]

While we do not share the deterministic orientation of Moore or Hartz, it is our contention that in terms of attempting to assess the influence of historical factors on political development, the understanding of the point of origin of the system is of crucial importance.

This appears to us particularly true in the case of Canada, where we contend that the political system that emerged in 1867 not only reflected the way in which major political problems facing the system were met, but also influenced the way in which future decisions on these problems were made.

If Canada is a federalist system, and the origin of that system is Confederation, then certainly much insight can be gained into explaining how various political problems have been dealt with over time by examining the decision which led to the adoption of that political system.

We believe that there has not been enough emphasis on explanatory research based on the premise that the union of the colonies was the result of decisions reached by a political elite. This elite collectively made decisions that served the political ends they considered best suited the needs of the British North American colonies at that time. Advocates of Confederation put forward these plans and ideas amidst the dissonance of criticism from those who opposed the idea or who clashed with the proponents on personal or political grounds. Thus, personal animosities, rhetorical arguments, and all the nineteenth century elements of disputation formed a part of the politics of Confederation. Nevertheless, out of this came not only the proposed union, but also the distinct political institutions of a federal political system.

The various political actors who dominated Confederation have been described in biographies and other historical studies which show their particular influence on the event.[8] Much of this work is excellent, but little scholarly work has been done in the way of a close analysis of the political attitudes which this elite as a whole held towards Confederation and federalism. Furthermore, many general theses have been advanced about the causes of Confederation, and each to a degree has been empirically verified by the evidence available. We certainly agree that this literature has clarified in many ways the nature of antecedent events on the decision.

Having decided to emphasize the political nature of Confederation, it became necessary to devise an appropriate focus for our research within the analytical literature on Canadian federalism. In looking at this literature, we were struck by what we have already described as the tendency to only consider federalism after it had become the operational system of government.[9]

One major approach in this vein is the legal-constitutional focus. K. C. Wheare, for example, discusses the balance of central and provincial powers, and concludes that the BNA Act, at best, provides for a "quasi-federal" form of government, owing to the preponderance of central power.[10] R. L. Watts follows the legal-constitutional model, and in his frequent use of Canada for comparative purposes, refers to the Wheare interpretation.[11] R. MacGregor Dawson's *The Government of Canada*, which for so long stood unchallenged as the standard work on Canadian government, adheres strongly to the legal-constitutional approach,[12] as does J. S. Mallory's more recent work, *The Structure of Canadian Government*.[13]

Another approach to federalism was introduced by W. S. Livingston, who developed the idea of a "federal society", emphasizing the social characteristics of the communities rather than their formal political institutions.[14] Michael Stein likewise explores the idea of federal political systems and federal societies, pointing out that in the Canadian case ethnic and linguistic differences are characteristic of a society which is federal in nature, and, according to Stein, "it is likely that conflicts will arise which will translate themselves into federal political problems".[15] Arend Lijphart's pioneering work on consociational democracy shares a similar perspective. Lijphart, however, concentrates on the role of elite accommodation in the integrative process within federal societies.[16] This idea was transposed by S. J. R. Noel, into a Canadian working model, which focuses on the relationship between political elites at the two levels of government and the way in which they relate to their particular mass constituencies.[17] Kenneth McRae's volume, *Consociational Democracy*, attempts to integrate the Canadian political experience into the general literature on consociationalism.[18]

Related to the concept of a federal society is the question of the relationship between a federal system and political behaviour. In this regard, the work of William Riker, *Federalism: Origin, Operation, Significance*, is an important contribution which stresses the role of political parties in the federal process. Having argued that the original bargain is determined through compromise between the competing interests of the elites who conduct the negotiations for union,[19] he turns later in his work to the role of political parties in affecting the degree of centralization which is achieved.[20] Among the many Canadian authors who have similarly focused on the impact of the party system are E. R. Black,[21] Alan C. Cairns,[22] and Denis Smith.[23] In their excellent work, *Political Parties and the Canadian Social Structure*, F. C. Engelmann and M. A. Schwartz refer frequently to the symbiotic relationship between the federal system and political parties.[24]

While traditional writing on Canadian federalism has concentrated

on the central government and its development, Cairns and Black
have made an important contribution by reminding us that Confederation put in train, not only a nation-building process, but just as
importantly it instigated a province-building process.[25] In recent years
greater attention has been focused on the importance of provincial
views of federalism, and especially those which emanate from Quebec.
Statements by provincial leaders now constitute an important part of
the literature on Canadian federalism. Professor Black has described
the various models of federalism which have achieved some acceptance in Canada along a continuum of national versus provincial
loyalties.[26]

This leads us into a fourth, and for our purposes final, approach to
federalism, that which focuses on the policy process. Donald V. Smiley has written so widely and with so much impact on interpretations
of Canadian federalism that he could have been justifiably included
in any of the previous three categories. However, it is his focus on the
policy process which we believe best defines his work. This orientation
is represented in his latest book, *Canada in Question: Federalism in the
Seventies*, by his third chapter, entitled "Executive Federalism", which
he defines "as the relation between elected and appointed officials of
the two levels of government", on matters of policy.[27] Indeed, his
analysis of the Riker thesis in the context of what he considers to be
the realities of Canadian politics, leads Smiley to say that "political
parties are thus of decreasing importance in the Canadian federal
system".[28] In Meekison's *Canadian Federalism: Myth or Reality?*, a
number of articles are reprinted which deal with "co-operative federalism", which is a term widely used to describe federalism that deals
with policy processes. Of these, the works of Edgar Gallant and R. M.
Burns are especially important.[29] A new and recent departure in the
literature dealing with the policy process has been Richard Simeon's
study of federal-provincial diplomacy, where he examines the "diplo-
matic negotiations" involved in the areas of constitutional change,
pensions, and financial arrangements.[30] With the exception of Simeon's work, which attempts to examine federalism based on the
attitudes of important federal and provincial actors, all others are
bound by essentially institutional perspectives and strictures.

We reiterate that the majority of these works on Canadian federalism appear to us to look at the outcroppings of a well established
edifice, without examining very closely the foundations of the structure. To continue the construction metaphor, what is visualized as the
outer dimensions depends both on the foundation and the inner con-

figuration of compartments. In other words, the origin of a structure, even if it is a concept of the mind, will of necessity have a rational link with the development of the structure itself. Perhaps the fundamental nature of the origin of a system is just as important as what the origin provides. Indeed, a concept which is crucial to the contention of the "two nations theory", is based on the particular interpretation of the intent of the actors involved in the Confederation agreement. Consequently, we believe that questions, such as the effects of stresses and strains on the political structure produced by a changing environment, may only be understood in their totality by investigating the basic design. While this language is metaphoric, it essentially points out the importance of our approach in the context of other studies of Canadian federalism.

In this work, therefore, it is by treating Confederation as a dependent variable, that we attempt to understand how a federal system came into being in Canada through an examination of both the environment of the time and the way in which a crucial political elite actually perceived that environment. We start by looking at the political system from the inside, using the point of origin of the system as the conceptual framework. With this rationale, we have embarked on our study of the decision in the Province of Canada leading to Confederation.

CHAPTER TWO

Research Framework

The focus of this work is an empirical study of Confederation, that is, of the decision by a political elite in the mid-1860s to adopt a federal system of government for the British North American Provinces. Confederation, of course, was not the result of a single decision, but rather the culmination of a long series of incremental decisions made by a number of different political elites both in British North America and in Great Britain.[1] While there are a number of ways to study this decision-making process, we have decided to break into the process at one critical point and subject this one decision to rigorous examination. The event in the decision-making process on which we have focused our attention is the debates in the Canadian Parliament on the Quebec Resolutions, which occurred during February and March of 1865,[2] and which led directly to the dispatch of a committee to London to negotiate the document of Confederation.

In studying decision-making, scholars have noted the important distinction between the "operational environment" and the "psychological environment". These concepts are explained by Harold and Margaret Sprout as follows:

> ... environmental factors become related to the attitudes and decisions which comprise a state's foreign policy only by being perceived and taken into account in the policy-forming process. The statesman's *psychological* environment (that is, his image, or estimate, of the situation, setting, or milieu) may nor may not correspond to the *operational* environment (in which his decisions are executed). But in policy-making, as we have stressed before, what matters is how the policy-maker imagines the milieu to be, not how it actually is.[3] [Italics in original.]

In an important theoretical article on decision-making, Michael Brecher, Blema Steinberg and Janice Stein have constructed a model of decision-making. They differentiate, among other things, the "operational environment" which defines the setting in which decisions are taken, and the "psychological environment" composed of the elite's "attitudinal prism" (i.e., a set of psychological predispositions based on a combination of societal and personality factors) and elite "images" (i.e., the actual perception of the operational environment on which the decision-maker operates, whether or not the perception is correct).[4] Simplified for our purposes, the model can be shown as follows:[5]

FIGURE 2:1   Model of Decision-making Process

OPERATIONAL ENVIRONMENT   PSYCHOLOGICAL ENVIRONMENT

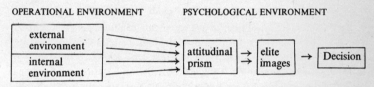

In order to apply this model to the decision leading to Confederation, we need to investigate three distinct areas: 1) the operational environment, 2) the "attitudinal prism", and 3) the "elite image" of the psychological environment.

With respect to the operational environment, a review of the historical literature of the Confederation period reveals four major reasons which may have been influential in shaping the decision of this particular political elite to consider a federal union of the British North American provinces as necessary in the 1860s. Three of these reasons, cultural factors, political factors, and economic factors, emerged from the internal environment, while geopolitical factors pressed upon the decision-makers from the external environment. Both the internal and external environments in which our decision-makers operated are reconstructed from the historical literature in the following chapter.

With regard to examining the psychological environment, it is necessary to try to get into the minds of the relevant political elite. While there were a number of distinct political elites which entered into the decision-making process, we have chosen as our elite the Parliament of Canada which decided upon the Quebec Resolutions as the basis for a new federal political system. Accordingly, we selected a sample of those members of Parliament who actually entered into the debate.

The Canadian Parliament was divided into two houses, the Legislative Council, composed of 69 members (21 life members and 48 elected members), 37 of whom actually participated in the debates;

and the Legislative Assembly, composed of 130 elected members, 76 of whom made their positions known, at least to some extent, in the debates. The primary criterion for inclusion in our sample was the degree of participation in the debates, operationalized as follows. Initially, we checked the *Debates* index for all participants whose total contribution reached at least ten pages. Following this, we re-examined the index for speakers who, although falling short of the ten-page minimum, nevertheless, had at least one speech which was at least eight pages in length. By employing these procedures we arrived at a sample of 41 members of the Canadian Parliament, 10 from the Legislative Council and 31 from the Legislative Assembly who participated in the debates. This represents 38.5 per cent of the legislators who actually spoke in the debates. Further, we checked our sample for adequacy on two crucial dimensions: the number of speakers from Upper Canada and Lower Canada (20 and 21 respectively), as well as the number of speakers voting in favour of or against Confederation (24 in favour, 15 opposed, and 2 recording no vote). (See Appendix.)

While it is virtually impossible to reconstruct a "prism" which accurately reflects the personality traits of our political elite, it is nevertheless possible to provide data on various factors which may have been important forces in its socialization. For as Donald R. Matthews has argued,

> The conviction that the political decision-maker's behaviour and decisions are influenced by his personal life experiences not only has a long and honourable history but is also substantiated by modern psychological and sociological research.[6]

Following is the list of theoretically important variables of a social, cultural, or political character which may have been influential in shaping the attitudes of the political elite toward the issue of Confederation.[7]

While a reconstruction of an "attitudinal prism" remains at best partial, the actual "images" which our elite held regarding Confederation are far more amenable to empirical verification. Employing the technique of content analysis to the speeches of our sample debating the merits of the Quebec Resolutions, we hope to be able to reconstruct the major reasons advanced by the political elite, both in support of and in opposition to Confederation. Furthermore, we will be able to correlate each of our socialization variables with support for or opposition to Confederation, in order to discover the impact of these variables on the elite images surrounding Confederation.

1. House   Legislative Council
                                          Legislative Assembly

2. Type of Constituency   Rural
   (Legislative Assembly only)   Mixed
                                          Urban

3. Type of Appointment   Elected Member
   (Legislative Council only)   Life Member

4. Member of the Government   Member of "Great Coalition"
                                          Non-member of Government

5. Region*   Upper Canada
                                          Lower Canada

6. Age

7. Country of Birth   Lower Canada
                                          Upper Canada
                                          England
                                          Scotland
                                          Ireland
                                          other

8. Age on arrival in Canada
   (for those not born in
   Canada)

9. Ethnic background   English
                                          Scottish
                                          Irish
                                          American
                                          French
                                          other

---

* The old Provinces of Upper Canada and Lower Canada became Canada
  West and Canada East at the time of the Union in 1840. However, they were
  referred to as Upper Canada and Lower Canada in the Quebec Resolutions
  debated in 1865, and for the most part were called by their former names
  by the debaters. We have done likewise.

10. Primary language	English
	French

11. Religion	Roman Catholic
	Protestant
	other

12. Occupation	Legal Profession
	Journalists/Editors
	Businessmen
	Farmers
	other

13. Party Affiliation	Lower Canadian Reform
	Upper Canadian Reform
	Lower Canadian Conservative
	Upper Canadian Conservative

In using content analysis to reconstruct elite images, we are of course aware of our critical assumption that what was said in the context of the debate accurately reflects the position of the particular political leader. While we acknowledge that other factors may have been present to lessen the validity of this kind of data to tap the dimension of elite images, it is our contention that verbal articulation aimed at clarifying one's position on such an important issue is indeed a reasonable indicator of one's actual position. Of course a good deal of work in the area of decision-making has been done on the basis of this very assumption, most notable the "operational code" formulation of Alexander L. George,[8] and the applications of the operational code to Dean Acheson,[9] John Foster Dulles,[10] and Lester B. Pearson.[11]

The development of a reliable scheme for coding the speeches proved to be a formidable task. We approached the problem pragmatically, developing and testing various coding procedures, both in terms of their adequacy in validly reflecting the actual content, as well as for inter-coder reliability.

We decided to employ the theme as our basic unit of analysis. The list of themes which we coded favourable or unfavourable to the proposed scheme of Confederation are grouped under the appropriate environmental categories as follows:

CULTURE: themes dealing with
1. harmonious relations between ethnic groups (will Confederation improve or worsen relations)
2. the general preservation of culture, religion, and laws serving the interests of the English-Canadian group
3. the general preservation of culture, religion, and laws serving the interests of the French-Canadian group
4. the following articulated "liberal fragment" values:[12]
   a. individualism (statements dealing with the the rights and protection of the individual)
   b. constitutional government (statements dealing with limited government, supremacy of law, due process, majority government and minority rights)
   c. social equality (statements dealing with equality of opportunity, social mobility, references to social classes and social status)
5. the following articulated "feudal fragment" values:[13]
   a. corporatism (statements stressing the primacy of the community over the individual and the group as the fundamental unit of society)
   b. authoritarianism (statements implying a hierarchical notion of society, veneration for certain institutions, e.g., monarchy and deferential attitudes toward authority)

POLITICS: themes dealing with
1. political deadlock (problems of the double majority system, poor administration, governmental instability, and references to partisan motives and bad faith on the part of opponents)
2. representation by population
3. nationalism (Confederation seen as a step towards nationhood, feelings conveying a sense of destiny of the aggregate, e.g., a "vast and great country")
4. mass public opinion (the fact that Confederation was to result from a legislative decision as opposed to some manifestation of popular support)
5. the appointive principle as opposed to the elective principle with regard to the method of selection of the Upper House
6. Confederation seen as a compromise to a Legislative Union
7. Confederation of just Upper and Lower Canada, not including other colonies
8. the proposed distribution of power between the federal and local governments

  9. the proposed distribution of power between the provinces
 10. the inability of Parliament to amend the Quebec Resolutions in any way
 11. appropriateness of timing

ECONOMICS: themes dealing with
  1. matters of trade and commerce (including tariffs and the Reciprocity Treaty with the United States)
  2. general future prosperity
  3. railways
  4. costs of the proposed Confederation (amount of debt, distribution of debt and taxation)

GEOPOLITICS: themes dealing with
  1. defence policy against American invasion
  2. fear of annexation to the United States
  3. Canadian western development
  4. strengthening the Imperial connection

Since the reports of the comments of the members of the Legislative Council and Legislative Assembly are not broken down into paragraphs in the *Debates*, we used as our standard reference unit the column of the page. That is, we examined the speeches by individual column, and using a separate code sheet for each column, coded every theme in the above list which appeared in a context either favourable to or unfavourable to Confederation.[14] As the length of the total comments of speakers varied considerably (8 pages minimum to 61 maximum), we standardized our measurement of thematic content by expressing our findings as a percentage of the total number of columns in which a speaker mentioned a particular theme, in either a favourable or unfavourable context. Our measurement categories assessing the importance of various themes in a speaker's contribution to the debates are as follows:

Per cent of Columns In Which Themes Appear

0%	– no importance
0.1% to 10%	– passing comment
10.1% to 20%	– some importance
20.1% to 30%	– important
30.1% to 40%	– very important
40.1% and over	– extremely important

Because it was not uncommon for speakers to comment on more than one theme in a given column, and further, since a number of these themes often fell within the same major category of interpretation, (for instance, themes of political deadlock, mass public opinion, and appointment of the Upper House all referred to in a context unfavourable to Confederation in the same column), total themes within a major category could possibly exceed 100 per cent. Thus, in assessing the relative importance of these major input categories from the environment, we employed the following measurement categories:

*Per cent of Columns In Which Major Categories
of Environmental Inputs Appear*

0%	– no importance
0.1% to 25%	– passing comment
25.1% to 50%	– some importance
50.1% to 75%	– important
75.1% to 100%	– very important
100% and over	– extremely important

The dependent variables in all tables based on the content analysis found in the book will be reported in terms of percentage of total columns computed in one of the two ways explained above.

All coding of the speeches was done by the authors, operating in six two-man coding teams. Team coding assignments were allocated in such a way that whenever a particular speaker made more than one speech, different teams would be assigned to code the various speeches. The actual coding process was carried out by one of the members of the team reading aloud the reported comments, with the other member doing the thematic coding. In addition to this quantitative coding, we prepared a descriptive summary of the major lines of argument in each speech.

By working in pairs and employing the procedures outlined above, using the formula for intercoder reliability

$$C_1R_1 = \frac{2M}{N_1 + N_2}$$

as found in Holsti,[15] computed on two separate samples of speeches our combined aggregate coefficient of reliability for coding themes into major environmental stimuli was 84.6 per cent, while our coefficient of reliability for coding specific themes was 75.2 per cent.[16] In a further check on coding accuracy, prior to transcribing the material from our coding sheets to key punch forms, we compared our coding against our summaries, and whenever there appeared that their might be some coding error, we went back and rechecked the speech.

While no research technique is infallible, we believe that a carefully constructed and controlled analysis of the content of the *Debates* will enable us to reconstruct the psychological environment, that is, the way in which this extremely important political elite actually perceived the stimuli which were necessitating a change of constitutional arrangement. Moreover, we believe that from this examination of the elite images of Confederation, we will be able to establish with greater insight, the origin of a number of crucial problems of Canadian federalism.

When we refer to the problems of Canadian federalism, it is easy to fall into the habit of seeing politics as problem solving, that is as the search for solutions. However, we would insist that in dealing with genuine and fundamental political problems, there should be a recognition that the problems are in reality unsolvable. As Bertrand de Jouvenal has cogently argued, "the clashing of terms" in the constitution of a political problem accounts for its unsolvability.[17] If a political problem, a genuine and fundamental political problem, cannot be solved in the usual meaning of that term (that is, solved once and for all), it nevertheless may admit of a settlement. "By settlement, we here mean any decision arrived at, by whatever means, on the question which gave rise to the political problem."[18] Since it is impossible that all competing demands can be fully met, the compromise will lead to a heritage of frustration. Perhaps the value of a settlement is best measured by its durability.

Hence, as we have asserted in the theoretical justification offered for our approach, the point of origin of a political system, with its distinctive set of problems, is instrumental in determining the unfolding of the political process which is set in train by that initial instance of decision-making. So we see that the issues most vehemently debated in the Confederation debates can be seen as permanent problems for Canadian decision makers and they conform closely to what Donald V. Smiley has identified as the three axes of Canadian federalism,[19] namely, French-English relations, Canadian-American relations, and the relations between the central provinces and the peripheral ones. The inability of the Fathers of Confederation to provide more than an interim settlement of outstanding problems, such as English demands for representation by population, French fears for their cultural autonomy, the economic and political tensions between Canada and the United States, and the priorities of national economic development policy, has been duplicated since that time by successive failures of Canadian political leaders to effect "solutions" to these questions. For the settlements they did achieve were not long-term ones, not to speak of being final. Perhaps the word "failure" is inappropriate, since the temporary compromises invoked in the initial Confederation agreement were probably the best that could have been reached given the disparate ethnic, regional, and economic interests involved. Subsequent politicians have continued to be faced with this divergent set of interests which resisted any forces that might have created a stronger commitment to what might be considered more pan-Canadian interests.

Shall we see the day when it is no longer asked how Confederation can be maintained, but rather how it was maintained so long?

rational Environment

The decision to inaugurate a new political system in the mid-1860s occurred in an environment which was an important influence not only on the decision to press forward for Confederation at that particular time, but on the type of political system that was to emerge as well. For although Confederation was a political decision reached by a particular political elite, it was from this environment that various stimuli or inputs were filtered through the value structure of this political elite, and eventually led to the realization of Confederation in 1867.

Systematic studies of the political environment are not tasks which Canadian political scientists have found particularly inviting. Alan Cairns, for example, finds that modern introductory textbooks on Canadian government and politics have been somewhat remiss in not stressing environmental factors in their analysis of contemporary Canadian political activity. Further, where the environment did receive some attention in one recent text, the treatment was faulted by Cairns for not applying "any theoretically grounded criteria for deciding which environmental factors to include, or even a realistic simplifying theme capable of imposing order on chaos".[1] In this work we hope to meet Cairns' constructive yet demanding criticism by utilizing a formal model of decision-making, taking into account the environment, which we hope will increase the order and reduce the chaos in our analysis. Thus, following Brecher's model, we have found it analytically useful to focus upon both the internal and external environments. The internal environment has been broken down into three component parts: the cultural, the political, and the economic; while the external environment is analysed in terms of geopolitical factors. These aspects of the environment of course mesh very closely with factors that traditionally have been considered important in explaining Confederation.[2]

A. The Internal Environment: Culture

The cultural factors which distinguished Upper and Lower Canada during the quarter century before Confederation were of the kind which tended to polarize these two regions rather than to draw them together, although it would be an error to fail to see the extent to which there was a degree of convergence which made Confederation possible under the auspices of men such as Macdonald and Cartier.

Cultural differences concern beliefs, values and interests, whether we refer to culture in the wider anthropological sense (characteristics of the whole society) or culture in the narrower sense, conscious articulation of experience in systematic thought and declaration. The salient cultural differences between Upper Canada and Lower Canada were found in a) religious beliefs, values and interests, b) political allegiances, values and interests, and c) social and economic values and interests.

We shall discuss first the religious cleavages which have been held to underlie the other differences, though some qualifications must be made in the examination of this thesis. Secondly, differences in political perspectives are examined, particularly conflicting views about the meaning and implications of self-government. Thirdly, the different ways of life in the two regions, contrasting economic outlooks and values will be described. This last consideration takes us to the thin borderline that separates a purely cultural dimension from one which is specifically economic.

But there is a framework in which these dimensions must be examined. That is the historical situation which found two peoples living side-by-side: one of whom has gained title to the territory it controls through military conquest; the other, the vanquished, incapable of forgetting the date on which it lost its distinct political existence, even though that too was a colonial existence.

Conquered peoples have a long memory. Decades, even centuries, after the conquerors enjoy their triumph, in what may have been but an episode in the epic of imperialism, the vanquished hearken back to the time when they were free, at least of the yoke they now bear. As the history of the American South attests, the experience of being conquered is an important component of political culture. The past before the conquest is idealized; a character is attributed to the people which may have little to do with historical fact. A retrospective mission is assigned to a particular group and that mission is seen as being blocked or almost obliterated by the culture of the conquerors. A nostalgia for the ante-bellum or pre-conquest days persists.

The psychology of the conquered is exemplified in the attitudes of all strata of French Canadians in the period before Confederation. The triad of ethnicity, religion, and language formed the configuration of the French-Canadian character, though language did not play the paramount role that it came to play in the days of the Report of the Royal Commission on Biculturalism and Bilingualism. Being Roman Catholic of French ancestry was fundamental. The cleavages in the French-Canadian community at the time of the Rebellion of 1837 can be understood in terms of class differences, differences in political ideology (the radical *rouges* and the anti-democratic conservatives whose spokesman during the Confederation debates was, in fact, the former *rouge*, Cartier). The landmark work of Fernand Ouellet is an attempt to interpret the history of this period in socio-economic terms, a fresh approach to the period and a challenge to the hitherto predominant nationalist school.[3] Ouellet's work is one of the initiatives in uncovering the importance of class and occupational factors in explaining behaviour too often viewed in terms of overworked cultural formulas.

It is safe to say that the opposition to the *rouges* came from those who saw them as typical of the kind of anti-clerical liberal so plentiful in continental Europe, and so rare in Great Britain.[4] A program which was both liberal and "democratic" was bound to run counter to prevailing attitudes in French Canada for two reasons: the success of the former of these ideas would lead to the secularization of society and the neutralization of the influence of the Catholic church in all spheres of French-Canadian life, the advent of the latter idea would be seen as an importation of American ideology into a society of hierarchical traditions.

But cleavages aside, the more immediate causes of French-Canadian anxiety in the period preceding Confederation from a cultural viewpoint were found in the proposals of the Durham Report. Here was a frank, unequivocal design for ending ethnic distinctions as a source of social and political turmoil. The violent anti-Catholic writings of George Brown only added fuel to the fire, and George Brown has always had a reserved place as the *bête noire* of the French Canadians.[5] So the grand design of assimilation coupled with the attacks on their religion and their mores account for the apprehensions, on the cultural level, at least, of the French Canadians. While few supported annexation to the United States as an alternative, the popularity of the idea can be easily understood in terms of these apprehensions.

The conquered are obsessed with old memories and old grievances; the conqueror does not understand this persistence in reliving the past rather than acceptance of the present and the new order. Furthermore, it is characteristic of conquerors to believe that they have won, not just through force and cunning, but because their society is superior, and because their vision is more in tune with the spirit of the age than that of the defeated society. Hence the Anglo-Saxons were not unusual in their belief in the superiority of their way of life. The English-speaking peoples of Canada were products of that nineteenth century liberal optimism which saw the possibilities of commercial and industrial societies spreading throughout the world through free trade and the adoption of laissez-faire. They were proud that the principles behind this movement had been elaborated by the political economists of Great Britain and that their practice had been initiated in that country.

We do not need to accept some of the cliches purveyed by some historians as to the materialism of the English Canadian as opposed to the spirituality of the French Canadian to recognize that there were sharp value differences in the two sections of Canada. Generally, the values of liberal capitalist society were imported into Lower Canada and contrasted with more traditional views of political economy. These liberal values, however, had become prevalent in Great Britain in the eighteenth century, and were part of the English-Canadian tradition. It is a truism of Canadian history to say that the English Canadians were individualistic and the French Canadians were more communal. This difference in political culture was to play an important role in the discussions that led to the establishment of the Confederation.

If the polity were seen as a collection of individuals, perceived in terms that Bentham had popularized, and if universal suffrage were accepted, as Bentham had proposed (but not all philosophic radicals had accepted), then the majority should determine for the rest. Ramsay Cook has erroneously referred to the conflict between the differing conceptions of the two Canadas as a quarrel between Locke and Rousseau.[6] While Locke may very well stand behind Bentham with his advocacy of majority rule, the French-Canadian political philosophy owes nothing to Rousseau, who specifically refused to give political recognition to groups smaller than the whole. Yet it must be said that Rousseau did have an idea of confederation which was different

A5887

both from the Union and the Confederation. The corporate existence of the community more likely is rooted in medieval conceptions of social and political organization which had continued to influence Roman Catholic thought. The French-Canadian idea was sociological, basing itself on the concrete association, and not accepting an abstract starting-point which considered the individual apart from his connections.[7] Perhaps in a rough way, the French Canadians were aiming at a system of functional representation, the political recognition of group existence. The later flirtations with the corporate state idea and an estates general reveal the tenacity of this conception of social life in the French-Canadian consciousness.

Consequently, representation by population within the Union, regardless of how reasonable it may have seemed from the perspective of majoritarian rule, obviously could not be accepted as a basis for political reorganization by the French Canadians within what was, in fact, a unitary state. Of course, minorities who believe in majority rule in principle can be extremely cautious about invoking the principle when it is not to their advantage. The French Canadians, however, did not reject the majority principle within their own territory: to that extent they made their peace with individualistic political theory. But to accept the principle within the Union, within a unitary state, was to accept the idea of assimilation. The Upper Canadian embrace of secularism was an additional reason for resisting "rep-by-pop". Accepting the secular ideal would bring an end to public support of denominational schools. Perhaps the basic difference between the two cultures consisted in the assertion of the one group that population should be the only relevant factor in the distribution of political power, and the assertion of the other group that population by itself is an abstract criterion that fails to take into consideration qualitative variables which are extremely important in making a country what it is. For a contemporary parallel to the Canadian situation before Confederation, one might examine the way in which a demographic shift in Belgium from the period of French (that is, Walloon) dominance to the current Flemish dominance has led to the establishment of a federal state in that country.

We have seen that the religious difference between the two regions turned upon the acceptance or rejection of the idea of the secular society and the secular state. While the Roman Catholics of Lower Canada were not in favour of the church establishment in the British sense, they did feel that the church should control the school system, minority churches having control over their own institutions. In Upper Canada, those who attacked a church establishment, once defended by Bishop Strachan, were not necessarily hostile to religion. Egerton Ryerson, for instance, believed that denominational schools were not necessary to provide religious instruction, which could be given through the non-denominational schools. In a Christian society, the schools are not neutral. Moral teaching and influence will be present without denominational control of any kind. The secularism of nineteenth century Canadian society did not create a situation in which there was a moral void, requiring as Emile Durkheim maintained in France, later in the century, a lay morality, a scientific morality. Even George Brown, though he favoured a division of labour between chapel and classroom, never intended to eradicate all religious influence from the schoolhouse. Of course, when the overwhelming majority of a community accepts this notion of secularism and shares basic values and a relatively small minority objects, the majority principle is called upon to settle the matter. However, a principle which is defensible when one's co-religionists or co-believers are in the majority may not be one a person wants to use when they are in a minority situation.

Since these were issues of debate in the public forum, the religious controversies of the period lead us inevitably to examine the ways in which the political hierarchy was understood in the two cultures. After 1849, in conjunction with the progress of individualism, majority rule and the secularization of society, there is a weakening in Upper Canada of aristocratic or oligarchical conceptions of hierarchy. In their place one finds a functional conception more in conformity with modern liberalism. In contrast to this tendency, Lower Canada, no doubt because of the traditional subordination of the laity to the clergy in the governance of the Roman Catholic Church, was more prone to continue the traditional conception of hierarchy and to extend it into the political sphere. The radical *rouges* were aware that the battle against the power of the clergy was a necessary step towards political democracy since ecclesiastical hierarchy easily became a model for the political. This appears to be what Pierre Trudeau referred to, in a noteworthy article some years ago, when he interpreted the French-Canadian tradition as largely a rejection of democratic values.[8] This is not the rejection of majoritarian democracy as an operative principle of parliamentary organization. It refers to authoritarian attitudes on the part of both leaders and followers. Trudeau's judgment was undoubtedly a conclusion he came to after witnessing the Duplessis regime in Quebec.

The contrast between the two cultures, individualist on one hand, communal on the other, modifies the way in which they will understand the political structure. Conceive of a society as a collection of individuals and the direction of that society goes where the greater force impels it. Liberal individualism, at least in its earlier forms, was prone to think of men as isolated individuals, not as members of a class or of some ethnic group. The alternative to such a conception has always been a view of society as analogous to an organic whole, developing in continuity from its early roots (the tree analogy being particularly dear to conservatives). If this alternative develops a theory of democracy, it is more likely to be stated in terms of group self-determination or autonomy. The second notion allows for minority rights not as the rights of isolated individuals, but as the rights of the group. Thus, the first position maintains that only individuals have rights (majorities having more than minorities), and the second that groups primarily have them.

The political idea of majority rule, regardless of whether or not it provides for protection of minority rights, may not necessarily lead to "progressive" government since the majority may well be defending traditional institutions and practices against the onslaughts of a new economic ideology. Critics have pointed out often enough the non-progressive character of Lower Canada during this period, but some of them have equated being non-progressive with being unjust.[9] However, the norms of representative government are respected as long as minorities are not prevented from having adequate representation and from agitating for their views.

We find, indeed, the development of economic liberalism in Canada alongside that of political liberalism. If the adherents of economic development through co-operation between government and capital could be considered as more advanced because they saw the need for establishing a railroad network across the country, they were not, for the most part, more advanced by the standards of avant-garde political liberalism. In France in 1848 a system of universal suffrage replaced the suffrage determined by property qualification. Almost twenty years later the leaders of the Great Coalition in Canada were still opposed to universal suffrage. On the other hand, the most unequivocal defenders of liberal democracy in Canada were the *rouges*, a political party noted for its mistrust of the proponents of economic development. Like their counterparts in Great Britain, the economic liberals in Canada after 1849 tended to resist democratization of the franchise. We do not find, moreover, a competition between the two major political alignments for the support of the working class as occurred at roughly the same time in Great Britain.

To sum up, the political rhetoric of this period indicates that democracy, radical democracy meaning universal suffrage, was still viewed with alarm. In this respect the weight of Canadian opinion, or better the weight of those who influenced opinion, stood with those liberals, like John Stuart Mill, reluctant democrats at best, who feared the effects of the "tyranny of the majority", if the lower orders were enfranchised. This kind of democracy was considered, negatively, as an American product at a time when most Canadians were particularly interested in distinguishing themselves from their neighbours.

Canadian liberalism, as expressed by the leaders of the Reform Party of Upper Canada, defended majority rule and was unwilling, as evidenced by the religious school question, to recognize the "rights" of a minority to its own school system. Liberals later made the concession of religious schools, not because of any change in conviction, but because of the situation of English Protestants in Lower Canada as a minority group. Consistency should have led to a cry for the secularization of education throughout the country, but since that was unlikely to be accepted in Lower Canada, the compromise on religious minorities seemed the only way out.

The period, then, marked a conflict between new claims and old customs. It was less a dispute about a respect for the norms of representative government than it was a difference about economic development. A dynamic commercial minority might very well feel oppressed because those who supported a stationary economy raised obstacles to its conception of what public policy should be. But such economic obstruction is not political oppression. At a later date the partisans of economic development prevailed. A consistent criticism of the conservative positions of the French majority in the 1830s would be simply that it was conservative and non-progressive, not that it took away liberties which were, in point of fact, *new* claims, *new* demands to change the status quo.

Now, if English liberalism was a defence of majority rule, though not necessarily of democracy, in an atomized society where groups as such received no recognition, it had the alternative either of denying political rights to a certain category of the people in order to establish a progressive majority (let us call this the Durham solution) or of establishing a larger unit in which a progressive majority would be in power. The latter was the implied result of Brown's cry for representation by population. Certainly liberals are not always faithful to their principles, any more than other people, and a pragmatic silence about the majority principle when it is disadvantageous may be suddenly followed by an appeal to principle when numbers shift. After all, the liberal idea of representation by population was not the war cry of a minority but that of a new majority. No matter how committed one might be to the majority principle, it is hardly something to be invoked when one is in the minority. While the principle of majority rule is accepted without difficulty in a homogeneous collectivity, it no longer has the same legitimacy when the collectivity is heterogeneous.

The clash between the economic liberalism of the English Canadians and the feudalism of Lower Canada has been the subject of innumerable commentaries and a strong link in Hartz's two fragment theory.[10] Hartz wants to show the durable aspects of a culture at the time that the culture breaks from the mother country. His thesis also seems to entail a belief in the relative impermeability of the cultural fragment. Some of the characteristics which are called feudal might be called pre-feudal or not necessarily feudal. For instance, the authoritarian notion of the Roman Catholic Church preceded the development of feudal society and outlasted its demise. While the part of the theory which concerns the liberal fragment has much to recommend it, Hartz's theory about the feudal fragment appears to have little value either as an explanatory or an evaluative factor in understanding the behaviour of French-Canadian society in the nineteenth century, for a feudal system involves more than a certain form of property title.

And in fact the system of feudal tenure, the seigneurial regime, was in decline, and there was considerable agitation, beginning in the 1840s for its abolition. There were some who clung to it as an element of *la survivance*, but more practical questions seemed uppermost and impeded the abolition, notably the matter of compensation. What is remarkable in the arguments brought forth by the owners of these feudal lands, as Fernand Ouellet has observed, is that the appeals by the seigneurs are not expressed in terms of prescriptive right, as one might expect, but in terms of a claim to one's property as a human right, a right of man. "Their conception was inspired by the theoreticians of the school of natural right, forgetting that the latter had condemned feudal property".[11] This is a significant indication of how deeply fundamental liberal ideas of property had penetrated into the thinking of the supposedly least liberal class.

How deeply then were feudal attitudes rooted in the French-Canadian consciousness? Alongside the traditional agricultural society, soon to be a complete system of freehold supported by the church for its promotion of personal and family virtue, there was a burgeoning commercial society centred at Montreal. At the same time, a new class of *notables* came to power throughout French Canada. These two developments established grounds of common interests between the bourgeoisie of Upper Canada and the new classes of Lower Canada.[12] Thus, across the barriers of religion, competing conceptions of social existence and different economic philosophies, there was developing an area of agreement in regard to commercial development and the possibility of class solidarity. Professor Careless, stressing the contrast between elements of convergence and elements of cleavage, says "this was the irony of the union in the 1850s: that while railways, commercial prosperity and rapid economic growth were binding its two Canadian communities ever more closely together, powerful cultural and social forces were rising to drive them angrily apart".[13]

B. The Internal Environment: Politics

The political environment which emerged from the cultural duality in the Province of Canada in the early 1860s was one of deadlock, frustration, and instability. According to R. MacGregor Dawson, "from 1841 to 1867 there were no less than eighteen different Cabinets in office",[14] the average tenure of a government being one-and -one-half years. By the time of the great political crisis of 1858, dubbed the "double-shuffle", the capability of the system to handle political problems was seriously in question. Increasingly, Confederation was advanced as one possible way out of the morass.

The Act of Union of 1840, which brought together in a unitary state the colonies of Upper Canada and Lower Canada, came about as a direct result of the Rebellion of 1837 and the recommendations of Lord Durham, who assumed complete control of the province of Lower Canada when the Constitution of 1791 was suspended.

Two divergent principles were intertwined in the establishment of the government of the Canadas. The first was the colonial principle, which installed a colonial governor with an executive council as the representative of Great Britain, the governor accountable to the British Parliament. The other principle was that of parliamentary supremacy, with the corollary of the subordination of the executive to the legislature. In the absence of political theorists or men of ideas, the apparent contradiction between these two principles could only be overcome by a politics of accommodation practised by pragmatic politicians as individuals and in groups. The Rebellion of 1837 signified the failure of accommodation. On one side, the dispute has been explained in terms of Great Britain's unwillingness to release colonial control, to work out a new and more flexible relation with its dependencies. On the other, Papineau and Mackenzie have been blamed for their republican fanaticism and their un-British refusal to compromise. The latter criticism is reminiscent of Burke's admonitions to the (colonial) contestants of the 1770s to leave aside discussion of rights and look to interests. This attitude is based on the assumption that muddling through can be a consistent policy rather than an occasional expedient. There comes a day when even political reason can take no more. That day came with the deadlock of the 1830s. To have called upon Papineau and Mackenzie to compromise would have been to repeat Burke's vain exhortations. It would, in addition, have been a counsel to capitulate.

The ninety-two resolutions passed by the Assembly of Lower Canada in 1834 constituted a sort of Declaration of Rights. One of its key proposals was for an elective legislative council in place of the one then existing, which was appointed. This move was to insure the independence of the legislative council from the executive council. As we know from Head's instructions,[15] the British government was unwilling to make constitutional changes. The Assembly's main weapon in aid of their bill of grievances was the refusal to vote supply. The British plan expressed in Russell's Resolutions, 1837,[16] was to circumvent the Assembly on supply, a rejection of the claim of the Assembly to exercise control over the executive through control over the powers of the purse.

The kind of changes the Assembly wanted would have entailed supremacy for it, and hence control over the executive. The position of the imperial authorities was that responsible government was incompatible with the status of a colony. A significant factor in the Melbourne administration's resistance to change in the government of the Canadas was the mercantilist trade policy as well as the pressures for political change in Great Britain, which had reached a climax in 1832, and had by no means yet slacked off. There were still agitators, radicals, who wanted to eliminate the House of Lords as being either mischievous or superfluous, to use Benthamite language. For some, then, the elimination of an appointed Legislative Council came very close to suggesting the superfluous state of the Upper House in Westminster.[17] The determination of Papineau's patriotes and the errors of the Imperial authority resulted in the traumatic Rebellion of 1837. Ged Martin, in a recent study of the influence of the Durham Report on colonial policy, puts the problem this way: "By demanding control of expenditure, and an elective upper chamber, the French radicals were in effect asking for the creation of a second independent government in the Empire".[18]

Mackenzie as well had taken up the revenue issue in his fight with the colonial regime. He inveighed against the politics of the Tories in the 1830s, which refused to make the executive subject to the assembly. He was in strong opposition to the governor and to the Family Compact and was repeatedly expelled from the assembly after being duly elected.[19] Mackenzie succeeded in making reform look dangerous. "Moderate republicans were unwilling to accept what appeared to be the radical American program that Mackenzie was beginning to advocate".[20] Yet the Assembly of Upper Canada also wanted men in the executive who had "the confidence and support of the Assembly".[21] Mackenzie, unlike most, decided on rebellion.

The superlatives often accorded to the Durham Report, while not unwarranted, tend to hide aspects which marred it. The remedy proposed was not offered in the spirit of conciliation which had marked Edmund Burke's interventions during the American crisis. The Report is a mixture of enlightenment and ethnocentric presumption, judiciousness and partiality. When one examines the Durham tenure in Canada and the ideas and dispositions of his advisors, this result is not surprising.[22] The Report's combination of a proposal for the establishment of responsible government alongside the notorious recommendation for the anglicization of French Canada reveals political perspicacity flawed by the liberal vision of the homogeneous society.

There are three major assumptions behind the Durham Report: 1) the conviction of the superiority of English culture and English political institutions; 2) the conviction of the inferiority of the French Canadians as a people and of French culture and institutions (excepting the French Church for what are probably pragmatic reasons); and 3) the belief in the progressive nature of capitalism and the need for the state to subsidize and support projects for economic development (roads, canals, railways, etc.).

As Pericles exhorted the Athenians to be moderate with their empire, so the Durham Report called for a reasonable policy of the imperial government towards its dependencies. The Durham Report breathes the confidence of Great Britain in its Imperial mission, its Imperial duties (for instance, in education), and, at the same time, reveals a refusal to understand why other peoples might want to preserve their own traditions and folkways, no matter how backward they might appear to the enlightened. Edmund Burke had suggested the dilemma of imperialism when he said that India should be ruled on its own principles. Why then should it be ruled by someone else? Durham's avowal of British superiority is striking in our time when such feelings must be masked.

It is not anywhere a virtue of the English race to look with complacency on any manners, customs or laws which appear strange to them; accustomed to

form a high estimate of their own superiority, they take no pains to conceal
from others their contempt and intolerance of their usages.[23]

The superiority of the English people consists in their "political and
practical intelligence".[24] Durham singles out for praise English municipal institutions, and he suggests that they be imitated. The English
are progressive, energetic, accustomed to self-government (responsible
government). English enterprise leads to prosperity. The English have
property and the intelligence to know what to do with it. In industry,
he speaks of "their own superior energy, skill, and capital".[25]

The superiority of the English is innate (racial). It is demonstrated
in the economic and political spheres, in the former because of the
enterprise of the English-speaking peoples, Americans included. In
politics, through the idea of self-government with responsibility at the
national level and municipal government at the local level, they are
an example for others to follow.[26]

As a consequence of this superiority, it is obviously right that the
inferior peoples accept the wise lead of Great Britain, its nurture, until
such time as they are fit for self-government. As John Stuart Mill was
to say later, in a passage in which the Durham Report was mentioned,
"there are, as we have already seen, conditions of society in which a
vigorous despotism is in itself the best mode of government for train-
ing the people in what is specifically wanting to render them capable
of a higher civilization".[27] Such a theory followed logically would
consider colonial domination as a mandate or trusteeship with the
responsibility of preparing the dependencies (subject peoples) to govern themselves. Because the French Canadians have shown themselves to be a non-progressive people, not capable of self-government,
they must continue to be subjected to the control of English Canada,
a project which requires a reorganization of government to ensure
that the English are in the majority.

So it is an assumption of the Durham Report that the French
Canadians are an inferior race. The Report notes, though without
approval, "a remarkable equality of properties and conditions" in
Lower Canada.[28] The French Canadians are conservative; they want
to maintain their distinct culture. The French Canadians have neither
institutions nor "character" comparable to those of the English. Public
services are neglected in the colony because they are underfunded.
The Report refers to the "ancient and barbarous laws" of the French
Canadians.[29] Again the main impediments to progress and prosperity
are "the backward laws and civilization".[30] These expressions undoubtedly pointed at the remnants of the feudal system and the

Report echoes the standard liberal criticism of the obstacles to complete alienability of property in this feudal system, residing in entailments and other encumbrances attached to the transfer of property. There seems little doubt that the Report exaggerates the extent to which such obstacles continued to exist. There are contemporary reports which paint a rather different picture.[31]

But more fundamental than these weaknesses in the institutions and practices of Lower Canada is the cultural inferiority of the French Canadians. Their character is inferior and, one must presume, this means that they are racially inferior. The Report advocates the remedy as involving "the process of assimilation to English habits".[32]

The final solution to the French-Canadian problem consists in settling once and for all the national character of Lower Canada.

> ...it must henceforth be the first and steady purpose of the British government to establish an English population, with English laws and language, in this Province, and to trust the government to none but a decidedly English legislature.[33]

The French Canadians must abandon hope. They must accept their fate. The process might be best called the Louisiana Solution, for in that state, "the French language and manners bid fair, in no long time, to follow their laws, and pass away like the Dutch peculiarities of New York".[34] Durham's report is an expression of the liberal belief in the homogeneous society.[35]

Lastly, the Report assumes that capitalist enterprise is an engine of progress and that no obstacles to the successful march of English enterprise should be allowed to remain. The Report observes that over half of the valuable seigneuries are already owned by the English. But even where the English are dominant, there are insufficient public services (roads and schools, means of transportation). While expenditures in Upper Canada have led to a public debt, under-expenditure in Lower Canada has left a surplus. The Report envisages the use of the surplus for the country as a whole. Yet the capitalist assumption is not the classical economic liberalism of laissez-faire as it is often misrepresented by those who have not read Adam Smith. On the contrary, the Report sees the state and its policies as an instrument of economic growth, the secular arm of the economic system, constructing roads, canals and railways to facilitate economic development, and creating conditions attractive to investors. Letting-alone was definitely not considered to be the best policy.

These three principal assumptions coloured the political advice given to the imperial government. The proposed union would guarantee English dominance. A union could avail itself of the surplus revenue of Lower Canada to help Upper Canada. A federal system was rejected because the Report thought federalism meant that federal powers were derived from the member states and it was not about to accept such a contract theory. The legislative union would provide Canada with responsible government, but the Report rejected election as a means of manning the executive council. The monarchical principle had to be safeguarded. Rather it was hoped that the governor would co-operate with the assembly to avoid the unseemly disputes which had culminated in the troubles of 1837. In addition, "a good system of municipal institutions" should be established.[36]

Donald Creighton summed up the proposals thus: "in the Report, the two principal political philosophies of the Canadas are combined and reconciled".[37] He referred to the Tory idea of legislative union and the Reformers' penchant for local autonomy. Indeed, when one looks at the political history of the United Province of Canada, it is apparent that the recommendation of the Durham Report failed to provide the framework for political stability. This is reflected in the party system in the United Province.

In his study of the development of political parties, Professor Cornell has identified at least eight distinct groups operating in the political system of the United Province of Canada between the years 1841 and 1867.[38] By the time of the election of the fifth Parliament, in 1854, politics had taken on a distinctly Radical-Conservative dichotomy in both sections of the province.[39] In Lower Canada the division was between the *rouges*, the more radical of the old Patriot party of Papineau's day, and the *bleus*, the conservatives, who were joined by the more moderate of the reformers in 1854.[40] In Upper Canada the major division was that between the Clear Grit persuasion of reformer and the Liberal-Conservatives, again a coalition of conservative and moderate reform elements. Thus in both Lower Canada and Upper Canada the early reform groups which had championed the cause of responsible government had been pushed into alliances with the conservatives by the emergence of more radical groups on their left. Political control in the United Province of Canada was held by this coalition of essentially moderate conservative groups representing both Lower Canada and Upper Canada for the decade preceding Confederation, with the conservative faction gaining strength in Lower Canada, while the Clear Grits were in the ascendancy in Upper Canada.[41]

The major political issue confronting the political system during the first decade of its existence was the achievement of responsible government. Reform movements in both Lower Canada and Upper Canada pressured various governors general to acknowledge that support in Parliament was necessary for the continuation of a ministry in power. After a period of gradual evolution, responsible government was finally achieved in 1848 with the coming to power of the "Great Reform Ministry" of Baldwin and LaFontaine. In the words of Professor Careless, this ministry "had clearly taken office in direct consequence of its party majority in parliament".[42]

At roughly the same time as responsible government had been achieved, the political system was faced with challenges from the left, both in Lower Canada and Upper Canada. In Lower Canada the *rouges* emerged, espousing a program calling for universal suffrage, secularization of society, representation based on population and annexation to the United States.[43] In Upper Canada, the development of the Clear Grit faction which split off to the left of the Baldwin-Hincks reform group, as well as the development of an independent radical position under George Brown, undermined the basis of reform strength. In Upper Canada, representation by population was the program of particular appeal. While in 1841, the population of Lower Canada exceeded that of Upper Canada 650,000 to 450,000[44] making equality of representation palatable to the English-speaking province, by 1851-1852 the demographic balance had shifted in favour of Upper Canada, 952,000 to 890,000, giving rise to George Brown's first motion calling for representation by population in 1853.[45]

Representation by population as an issue became a symbol not only of English-French differences, but of western agrarian discontent with the alliance of English-speaking economic power in Montreal with French-speaking political power of the *bleus*.[46] Increased Upper Canadian pressure for representation by population was met by an equally strong resistance by the French-speaking segment of the population. These contradictory pressures created an impasse in a political system, which although unitary in form, had been virtually from the beginning dependent on a double majority principle for its operation.[47]

By the late 1850s, the system was clearly becoming inoperable. According to Waite,

> With goodwill and commonsense, and a recognition that the economy of the two sections was inseparable, the Union could be made to work. This was the view of Conservatives, east and west. But of goodwill there was little, and under the circumstances commonsense was a counsel easy to urge and difficult to realize.[48]

As a solution to the problem, by 1859, both the Conservative and Reform parties had put forth proposals for a federal system of government. The Conservative proposal, that of Alexander Galt in 1858, called for a federation of all British North American provinces, while the Reformers in the Great Reform Convention of 1859, preferred a federal system for the two Canadas only.[49] George Brown had managed to carry this position against those who wished the complete abolition of the Union as a means of achieving representation by population. For Brown the lure of expansion into the north west militated against the uncompromising search for reform.[50]

In the late 1850s and early 1860s as a consequence of the above problems, ministerial continuity was becoming more difficult to maintain within the double majority framework, in that while the Reform groups were increasing their numbers in Upper Canada, the opposite was occurring in Lower Canada.[51] Beyond this there were major partisan squabbles over administration of monies and resultant scandals.

The insistance on the part of Upper Canada Reformers on representation by population made difficult the cementing of an alliance with their counterpart radical group in Lower Canada, the *rouges*. The solution to this impasse was the construction of the Great Coalition of 1864, which saw George Brown, the leader of the Reform group in Upper Canada, join with the Upper Canadian Conservatives and *bleus* from Lower Canada "in order to alter the frame of the Canadian constitution and, provide, in the federal principle, a new field in which the legitimate aspirations of Upper and Lower Canada as a whole might be worked out by normal interplay of political parties".[52]

It was this government which invited itself to the Conference on Maritime Union held at Charlottetown, organized the follow-up Quebec Conference, and brought to the Canadian Parliament the Resolutions of the Quebec Conference as the basis of a federal political system.

C. The Internal Environment: Economics

Economic conditions at the time of the Confederation present a somewhat paradoxical picture. On the one hand, there existed rather widespread prosperity, but on the other hand the bases of this prosperity were endangered. Confederation was among other things an attempt to forestall the effects of those factors which threatened prosperity. Foremost among these was the loss of protected markets in Britain during the 1840s and 1850s and the imminent loss of the Reciprocity Treaty with the United States.

Before looking at the threats which faced Canada's trading relations, it is useful to review the nature of the Canadian economy as a whole at that time. The combined population of Upper and Lower Canada in the 1860s was approximately 2.6 million people.[53] Obviously then we are not discussing a country where population constituted a major economic advantage in terms of internal markets. There had been large scale immigration in the 1850s and 60s and by 1867 most of the useable and valuable agricultural land had been occupied. It was the attraction of economic opportunity which brought people from England where economic hardship was widespread.

Unfortunately many of the settlers, who were often sent to Canada through assisted emigration by the British government, lacked the skills and capital to make an immediate contribution to the Canadian economy. The likelihood was that those possessing these advantages would settle in the United States rather than Canada and this was one of the factors which contributed to a noticeable difference in the level of economic activity between the two countries. As one author put it, Canada in the 1830s and 1840s "became notorious for having poor business prospects and for attracting the less suitable type of settler".[54] Many of those who landed in Canada as immigrants were in reality just passing through to the United States. In addition, emigration of Canadians to the United States was assuming large proportions, and by the 1860s it was estimated that in the neighbourhood of half a million persons had left for the United States.[55]

All of this, of course, thwarted the growth of a large internal market and the prosperity which might accompany it. The existence of land speculation on a wide scale created problems for settlers which governments were unwilling to rectify. The Clergy reserves constituted the same kind of impediment to agricultural growth. Problems such as these were minimized in the United States which further enhanced its competitive advantage for immigrants. In addition to all of this the French-speaking population of Lower Canada was not really interested in being overwhelmed by large numbers of English-speaking immigrants and thus discouraged settlement in Lower Canada.

For those people who did stay in Canada, agricultural pursuits were predominant.[56] Subsistence farming was typical throughout the Canadas well into the nineteenth century. The growth of wheat as a staple, however, helped to change this somewhat in Upper Canada by providing disposable income. In Lower Canada, even during the 1860s, subsistence farming was still very widespread. The concomitant of this type of farming, of course, was the slow growth of trade since a major segment of the population was producing almost all of its own needs. This began to change when a number of factors combined to make the export of wheat to England both possible and profitable. In turn, this meant that more land could be brought into cultivation and specialization could take place. Thus manufacturing and trade could begin to develop as a result of the existence of a staple agricultural product.

All of this was threatened by the introduction of free trade in England in the 1840s which undermined Canada's competitive advantage. Fortunately, the combination of the Reciprocity Treaty with the United States, increased economic activity associated with railway building, and finally large American demand during the Civil War, took up the slack and indeed enhanced Canadian prosperity. In this light it is evident how important the impending abrogation of the Reciprocity Treaty was in the Confederation issue.

In addition to farming, other primary economic activities were most important. Lumbering was the chief among these.[57] It was well suited to become a key means of livelihood in the St. Lawrence valley for the forest resources were there and initially it took neither expensive machinery nor skilled labour to exploit them. As with wheat, Britain, of course, was the major market for lumber products. Here Canada faced the problem of transport for such a bulky product and the competition of the Baltic States. The mercantile system, until the 1840s, helped to deal with the latter problem. The conversion of wood into potash, a more easily transportable product, helped to ease the transportation problem.

The Ottawa valley became the centre of the lumbering industry since it contained extensive forest, there was less arable land than elsewhere, and the Ottawa River provided a major transportation route. Some large sawmills began to develop in the 1850s as the new railways opened hitherto inaccessible areas, and capital, often American, became available for new large-scale operations.[58] In addition, a ship-building industry developed at Quebec. This relationship of the lumber industry and ship-building, it might be noted here, was even more crucial for the economies of Nova Scotia and New Brunswick.

The end of the mercantile system was a serious blow to the trade in lumber as was the end of the era of wooden sailing ships. Reciprocity could and did have some positive effect on the lumber trade but it obviously could not do anything to cushion the results of the coming of the age of steam for the Canadian lumber industry. Thus lumber-

ing was an uncertain business which had to deal with resource deple-
tion, changes in technology, freight rates and tariffs and the result was
that after the 1850s the long term trend was downward.[59] Again, the
lack of a reliable internal market was a major problem where Canada
did not have any competitive advantage in international trade.

Fundamental changes in Canada's economic structure were occurring. The development of the staple trade and the rise in population,
especially in Upper Canada, led to the growth of towns in which
tradesmen and small manufacturing concerns could take advantage of
the fact that farm families were not making everything for themselves.
Gristmillers, blacksmiths, carriage makers, cabinet and furniture makers, boot and shoe makers and tailors and clothiers set up shop in the
towns and tended to sell their outputs almost exclusively in their own
localities. According to Leo A. Johnson in his study of the County of
Ontario:

> The villagers manufactured most of the products required by the local
> farmers, while farmers supplied the villagers with food, fuel and other
> agricultural products. In such an economic unit, the only exports were
> agricultural products, the only imports were raw materials for manufactur-
> ing and luxury goods.[60]

Some exceptions to this took place of course mainly in the larger
centres; for instance, cotton mills at Sherbrooke, a sugar refinery at
Montreal, railway and locomotive factories at Toronto and Kingston
as well as iron works and agricultural implement plants in a variety of
places.[61] None the less, the level of manufacturing activity was not
really high and most manufactured items of any sophistication continued to be imported.

Because of the export of primary products and import of manufactured items the commercial structure of Canada grew steadily in
importance. As the nineteenth century advanced, the almost exclusive
trade with Britain through the port of Quebec had to share its pre-
eminence with a growing trade with the United States especially after
the Reciprocity Treaty. Montreal emerged as the major commercial
centre, but Kingston and later Toronto also saw a rise in commercial
activity while the relative importance of Quebec declined. The whole-
salers with their connections outside the country controlled the local
merchants through the extension of credit.[62] In turn, the credit system
involved the farmers who were dependent on a yearly cash crop. A
banking system was in existence and the prosperity of that time led to
the creation of new banks which were not always well based. Often
their notes were discounted in other cities. In 1858 the decimal system

based on the dollar was introduced; a reflection of the growing influence of the United States rather than Britain in economic matters. The monetary system, however, was still far from well developed before Confederation and this constituted yet another barrier to the development of a vibrant economic system.

The growth of Montreal as a commercial centre, and the desire to buttress its position and make it prosper, further led to developments in the economic system which had wide-ranging consequences. By the development of the St. Lawrence navigation system through the creation of canals, it was hoped that Montreal could capture the export trade of not only the Upper Canadian hinterland but also of the American midwest.[63] The Erie Canal was diverting this trade to the port of New York, via Toronto. The Saint Lawrence canal system was built at a heavy cost to the public purse but did not prove successful. When in their turn, railways were planned to try to do what the canals could not for Montreal, they created serious rifts between those farming interests which sought only to have the cheapest means to export wheat and import manufactures and the commercial interests who sought to have the public treasury subsidize the emergence of the Montreal commercial centre. The result of this controversy was the creation of a more modern transportation system and the basis for a growing economic system. The cost, however, was a substantial public debt for a country like Canada. Of the debt which equalled seventy-five million by 1866, eighteen million had been incurred for the canal system and thirty-three million had gone into loans for railways.[64] The creation of the debt left a strong distrust of railroads in the farming community and a bitter relationship between it and the Montreal centred interests.

While the type of development discussed above was going on in Canada, some major developments of very wide ranging significance were taking place outside her borders. The first was the victory of the free trade policy in England, which ended the mercantile system, hitherto the basis for the economic system of Canada. A variety of factors cushioned the effects of this major change in Canada's economic environment. Among them was the Crimean War which prevented Russian competition for English markets. The building of railways also created needed economic activity. But more than anything it was the Reciprocity Treaty which allowed Canada to continue on a course of economic growth despite the loss of trade advantages with Britain. The Treaty allowed freedom of entry of almost all primary products. There were some tariffs which remained principally for revenue purposes, and when these were raised in 1853 and 1858 the United States charged that Canada was violating the spirit of the Treaty. Likewise the Americans were annoyed by the partial elimination of tolls on the St. Lawrence River canals which, they argued, put the Erie canal at a disadvantage. There were as well other disagreements about the provisions of the Treaty, but more generally, the strained relations between Britain and the United States over the Civil War made the abrogation of the Treaty in 1866 a foregone conclusion.[65]

Thus, while Canada was in a period of relative prosperity in the 1850s she faced the stark reality of having lost her competitive advantages with her two major trading partners. In addition, the attempt to capture for Montreal and the St. Lawrence system pre-eminence in overseas trade had achieved only limited success and had created a large public debt, whose existence was a major political problem. Canada had been unable to match the United States in economic growth and had thus not attracted as many, or as skilled, immigrants. This lack of population growth meant there was not the internal market that was necessary for industrial growth. Confederation was looked upon as a way out of these economic dead-ends which Canada faced in the 1860s.

D. The External Environment

The external environment is important to understanding the timing and character of Confederation in two major and interrelated ways. The first deals with Canada's relationship with the mother country, Great Britain, where changes in commercial policy, which resulted in removing tariffs and other restrictions of commerce beneficial to Canada, coupled with meagre defence commitments, were interpreted as having as their objective the pushing of the colony from the nest. The second deals with Canada's relations with the United States. Here, the American Civil War, with the difficulties this conflict created for United States–British relations, had the effect of underscoring Canadian vulnerability to American military attack in the east and expansion into British North North American territory in the west.

As mentioned in the discussion of the economic sector, the solution to the earlier disturbances from the external environment in the form of British free trade policies in the 1840s had been the Reciprocity Treaty with the United States entered into in 1854. However, by the early 1860s Canada was again experiencing stress from the external environment. This time the source was the United States where the Civil War had erupted in 1861.

The idea that the American Civil War was a major factor in promoting Canadian Confederation is well established in the literature. Take for example the following passage from a recently published text on Canadian foreign policy.

Present-day Canada took shape during the American Civil War, and under the threat—real or assumed—of an American invasion. That situation was used adroitly by the Fathers of Confederation to force agreement on the union of the British North American Provinces; otherwise, it might never have happened. The imperial authorities in London welcomed the plan because, among other considerations, it held the promise of reducing their military and financial commitments in North America, and concomitantly, the likelihood of another war with the United States.[66]

While scholars disagree whether public opinion in Canada initially favoured the North or the South,[67] it was not long before Northern antagonism against Great Britain over what was perceived to be a pro-Southern foreign policy had led to a serious deterioration in relations on the North American continent. As early as July 1861, Great Britain reinforced her small British North American contingent of 4,300 men by an additional 2,144.[68]

In November, 1861, the arrest and removal of two Confederate Commissioners travelling to Europe on the British steamer *Trent* nearly provoked war between Great Britain and the United States. Lord Monck, the Governor General of Canada, began making preparations for local defence, while Great Britain hurriedly sent additional reinforcements which by the following summer totalled 14,436 men.[69]

War with the United States was not of course a goal of British foreign policy. As C. P. Stacey has pointed out, Great Britain was at the same period in time faced with crises in Europe.

Historians have rightly recognized that it was military weakness that paralysed the action of the United Kingdom in Europe; they have failed to point out that that weakness was the more serious in that British statesmen had to face the fact that if compelled to fight in Europe they would quite probably find themselves fighting the United States in North America at the same time. The British Army was an inadequate instrument to deal with either of these emergencies singly; it was monstrously inadequate to deal with a war on two fronts, one on each side of the Atlantic, British policy has rarely if ever been faced with a more unpleasant dilemma.[70]

At the same time as both governments in England and Canada saw the need for defence of British North America, there was lack of agreement as to who should bear the financial responsibilities for this defence.

Colonies clearly had become somewhat anachronistic in an era of free trade. As P. B. Waite has pointed out, Britain could justify defence neither in terms of sources of raw materials nor markets. To make matters worse, Canada appeared reluctant to assume her share of the costs of colonial defence. When a militia bill calling for the appropriation of half a million dollars failed in the Canadian Parliament in the spring of 1862, Canadian credibility in London was shaken. "Whatever may have been the causes of the defeat in Canada ... the reaction in Britain was unmistakable. A Colony of two and a half million inhabitants that balked at a half million dollars for its own defence could not expect Britain to make extensive efforts".[71] Thus a major change in British attitudes toward Confederation had taken place between 1858, when a proposal for a federal union emanating from Canada had been met with quiet indifference[72] and 1864, when according to Waite, Confederation "had the positive, indeed ruthless backing of the colonial office".[73]

The military threat from the United States to the settled areas of Canada continued to arouse concern. Relations took a particularly nasty turn in the fall of 1864, when a group of Southern partisans using Canada as a base of operations crossed the border into Vermont and robbed three banks and killed a civilian in the village of St. Albans before fleeing back into Canada.[74] Although the perpetrators were arrested by Canadian authorities, when charges were later dismissed on a point of law, anti-Canadian opinion in the North flared to dangerous heights and General John A. Dix, Commander of the Military District of the East, ordered that in the event of future raids, his troops should "pursue raiders wherever they took refuge and under no circumstances to surrender prisoners to anyone before returning them to the United States, where they could be tried by martial law".[75] Control of the border was tightened on both sides. The United States instituted a passport requirement for travel into the United States, while Canada formed a special police force to monitor Confederate activities in Canada.

When the American Civil War ended in 1865 and no invasion of Canada materialized, still other hostile pressures were felt from the south. Most serious of these were the activities of the Fenians,[76] which took on an added significance with the large number of soldiers who had fought in the Civil War available for recruitment by the disgruntled Irish.

While the most visible threat from the United States during the Civil War years took the form of a possible direct military attack, the United States presented what was to some an even more formidable challenge to the future of British North America. This challenge was occurring in the west, where the coincidence of geography and transportation routes, immigration into Minnesota, and a British policy of neglect appeared to be working toward the eventual incorporation of the Red River Settlement into the political orbit of the United States.[77]

The period immediately prior to Confederation was one in which both Canada and the United States were looking westward. In Upper Canada the last open land in the Western peninsula was auctioned off in 1855.[78] In the United States, "between 1850 and 1860 population of the area that became Minnesota increased 2,730 percent".[79] Clearly, the manifest destinies were going to clash in the west, and schemes of Confederation, both in 1859 and 1864, were seen as ways of blunting the American initiative, while pushing the claim for a Canada stretching as a national entity across the Northern half of the continent.[80]

Thus the external environment affected the movement for Canadian Confederation in a number of mutually reinforcing ways. Increased United States belligerence toward Great Britain as a consequence of the American Civil War, which was sure to be visited upon Canada in the event of actual hostilities, led at the same time to pressures in Great Britain to cut losses in this vulnerable area, and to the necessity for political elites in Canada to contemplate their future condition.

In way of summary, Donald Creighton places the external factors contributing to Confederation in the following perspective:

It is easy to exaggerate the influence of the American Civil War upon the movement for Canadian Confederation. . . . The American Civil War did not inspire the Canadian desire for constitutional reform or the British wish for retrenchment; but it did help give both amplitude and urgency to the Anglo-Canadian plans for achieving their objectives.[81]

CONCLUSIONS

Thus an examination of the operational environment in Canada at the time of Confederation reveals that there were factors which promised a perpetuation of the divisions which had rent the country throughout the nineteenth century. At the same time, there were factors which provided a basis for co-operation between the two leading ethnic groups. The development of the country brought with it the need for new attitudes, new policies and the provision of political institutions capable of planning for the future.

The cultural differences between the two parts of Canada continued to be a divisive influence. These striking differences concerned the idea of a secular society opposed to one in which religion is given public recognition, the claims of ethnic groups, economic ideology and the diverse social attitudes prevalent in the union. The growth of capitalist enterprise was alarming to rural conservatism. Liberal individualism clashed with attitudes of social solidarity. Disagreements about the meaning of democracy were rife.

Yet, with all these differences, there were areas of agreement and co-operation. Political allegiances cut across cultural as well as class differences. Party loyalties changed as new political alignments were formed.

However, hopeful prospects for co-operation despite cultural differences were impeded by the working of the legislative union. The failings of this system stemmed from its origin. It was a scheme for fusion, when accommodation was what was needed. The subsequent series of short-term administrations, political deadlock, frustration and instability made it clear that a revision of the political system was imperative. But in examining the alternatives, the people of Canada had to reckon with the fact that the spectre of assimilation, raised by the Durham Report, remained present in the consciousness of French Canadians. The emergence of a two-party system (Conservatives and Reformers) did not break the deadlock. This only came about when Reformers joined Conservatives in the great coalition.

While the time of the Union was a period of relative prosperity, there were clouds on the horizon. The end of Great Britain's mercantile policy, friction with the United States, a heavy public debt and other obstacles to economic growth gave rise to apprehensions about the future. The increasing tension between Canada and the United States was also an important force in shaping Canadian attitudes, particularly at a time when the ties with Great Britain were slackening.

CHAPTER FOUR

The Political Elite:
Socio-political Characteristics

Turning from an examination of the operational environment to the psychological environment in which our decision-makers operated, the first dimension which we need to consider is the "attitudinal prism" of the political elite. The method by which we intend to probe this particular aspect is through an examination of the social political backgrounds of the elite.

While for many years the social backgrounds approach to elite studies operated on the assumption that social background categories were indeed related to attitudes and behaviour, Donald Searing and Lewis Edinger have systematically examined different background variables in order to appraise their utility in predicting political attitudes among elites in a number of political systems.[1] While their conclusions regarding the cross-national application of social background variables to predict attitudes are on the whole pessimistic, they do find that within the context of a particular political system there is a relationship between the two; however, some background variables are better indicators of political attitudes than are others. Among German and French elites, social class, age, occupation, and party affiliation seem to be the strongest predictors,[2] while in the United States, socio-economic status (occupation), age, religion, level of education, region, as well as political affiliation, appear to be the most potent predictors of political attitudes.[3]

We did not begin this research with any *a priori* assumptions regarding the relative importance of specific social and political background characteristics, nevertheless, a judgment had to be made regarding those which appear to be of particular relevance in the formation of political attitudes. These variables can be divided into two general categories: first, data dealing with the elites' legislative position, that is, whether an individual was a member of the Legislative Council or Legislative Assembly, whether he represented a constituency in Upper or Lower Canada, whether or not he was a member of the government. For members of the Council we examined the type of appointment (elected or life member), type of constituency represented for members of the Assembly, and party affiliation for all members. The second category includes demographic variables such as country of origin, age at which immigrants came to Canada, religious affiliation, ethnicity, age, primary language, and occupation.

With regard to the first of these categories, employing the criterion of length of remarks in the Debates (at least ten pages in total length or one speech of at least eight pages) we arrived at a sample of forty-one debaters, thirty-one from the Legislative Assembly and ten from the Legislative Council. Of the total membership of the Council, forty-eight were elected members while the balance of the sixty-nine were appointed for life. Our sample of the Legislative Council virtually mirrors this distribution, as 70 per cent were elected, while 30 per cent were life appointees. In the Legislative Assembly, of course, all 130 members were elected. In this case, we examined the constituencies which our sample of thirty-one members of the Assembly represented in order to ascertain the representativeness of the group with regard to the urban-rural composition of the country at the time. While we realize that members did not always live within the boundaries of the constituencies which they represented, we nevertheless assume that members were at least spokesmen for the interests of their constituents. Distinctions were made between rural, urban, and mixed rural-urban constituencies on the basis of the following criteria:[4]

Rural— a constituency which contained no city or part of a city with a population over 4,000.

Urban— a constituency which contained at least one city or part of a city with a population over 10,000.

Mixed— a constituency which contained at least one city or part of a city with a population between 4,001 and 10,000.

TABLE 4:1 Percentage of Members of the Legislative Assembly Representing Rural, Urban, and Mixed Constituencies

RURAL	MIXED	URBAN
64.5%	19.4%	16.1%

Looking at data in Table 4:1, as one might expect given the level of industrialization in Canada in the mid-nineteenth century, representatives from rural ridings predominate, accounting for roughly 65 per cent of the Assembly sample. The distribution does at the same time, however, point out the importance of the growing urban centres, as their spokesmen appear to take part in the debate on this important question in greater numbers than one would expect from examining the level of urbanization in the country as a whole.[5]

A further dimension, which cuts across both Council and Assembly is whether the members formed part of the "Great Coalition", the government which brought forward the Quebec Resolutions for adoption or whether they held no positions in the government. Here our sample consists of 19.5 per cent ministers of the government with 80.5 per cent non-members, giving us adequate representation in both categories.

As Paul Cornell demonstrated, during the period of the Union, politics was characterized by a Reformist/Conservative dichotomy, with each persuasion represented in Parliament by regional counterparts; the *rouges* in Lower Canada corresponding to the Reform-Liberals or Grits of Upper Canada, and the *bleus* of Lower Canada corresponding to the Liberal-Conservatives of Upper Canada.[6] As data in Table 4:2 show, our sample reflects this deadlock which had developed during the 1850s, with 48.8 per cent of the sample adhering to the Conservative persuasion while 51.2 per cent supported the Reform program. While these political groups lacked the strict party discipline characteristic of modern day political parties, Cornell argues that these groups were marked by internal cohesion and that this cohesion increased during the Union period.[7]

TABLE 4:2   Party Affiliation of the Political Elite

LOWER CANADIAN REFORM	UPPER CANADIAN REFORM	LOWER CANADIAN CONS.	UPPER CANADIAN CONS.
24.4%	26.8%	26.8%	22.0%

A final factor with regard to representation concerns which of the two constituent parts of the Province of Canada the selected debaters represented. On this question we find virtual balance, with 51.2 per cent representing Lower Canada, while 48.8 per cent represented Upper Canada. When one contrasts these respective percentages of seats with the actual populations of the two parts of Canada, (1,620,851 for Upper Canada and 1,191,516 for Lower Canada in 1871) one finds the same disparity which advocates of "representation by population" at the time used to support their demand. However, the distribution does reflect rather well the system of "double majority" which in fact had obtained legitimacy during the period of the Union.

Looking now at some of the major socializing factors which might have influenced the attitudes of our elite, we find as data in Table 4:3 indicate, that the bulk of our elite sample was between forty-one and fifty years of age at the time of the debates over Confederation. Significantly, the dates of birth of this cohort (between 1816 and 1825) have them reaching early manhood at a time when the international system experienced a period of protracted stability following the revolutionary upheavals of the Napoleonic period. Only 15 per cent of the sample were older than fifty years, while 22.5 per cent ranged between twenty-one and forty years of age.

TABLE 4:3   Age of the Political Elite in 1865

21-30	31-40	41-50	51-60	61 and over
2.5%	20.0%	62.5%	12.5%	2.5%

If we examine this age distribution according to which constituent part of Canada members of the elite represented, we see from data in Table 4:4 that the range in age of representatives from Lower Canada is greater (one member in the twenty-one to thirty age group and one member older than sixty-one), while in Upper Canada the concentration of members in the forty-one to fifty age group is even more pronounced, fully 75 per cent.

TABLE 4:4   Age of the Political Elite in 1865, by Upper and Lower Canada

	UPPER CANADA	LOWER CANADA
21-30	0	5%
31-40	15%	25%
41-50	75%	50%
51-60	10%	15%
61 and over	0	5%

The extremely important factor, country of origin, is reflected in data in Table 4:5 which indicate that 52.5 per cent of the elite were born in Canada, of which 32.5 per cent were natives of Lower Canada and 20 per cent were born in Upper Canada. A point of interest relevant to the degree of interaction between Canada and the Maritimes is that no member of the sample was born in the Atlantic Colonies. The most significant group not born in Canada, were those born in the British Isles, who accounted for 37.5 per cent, with the remainder born either in Europe or the United States.

TABLE 4:5	Country of Birth of the Political Elite				
LOWER CANADA	UPPER CANADA	ENGLAND	SCOTLAND	IRELAND	OTHER
32.5%	20.0%	10.0%	15.0%	12.5%	10.0%

Since nearly half of the sample is non-Canadian by birth, the age at which these members immigrated to Canada assumes considerable importance, for literature on political socialization suggests that basic political attitudes are firmly established by adolescence if not earlier.[8]

TABLE 4:6	Age at which Immigrants came to Canada			
0-5	6-10	11-15	16-20	20 and over
22.2%	11.1%	11.1%	22.2%	33.3%

Data in Table 4:6 reveal that 55 per cent of the non-native born sample had not immigrated to Canada prior to their sixteenth birthday, indicating a substantial input of British political values in the attitudinal prism of the elite. If we consider as well the picture of the ethnic backgrounds of the total sample, the potential influence of the British political tradition appears even more important, as data in Table 4:7 indicate approximately 65 per cent of the sample were descended from Anglo-Saxon stock, the French accounting for the vast majority of the balance.

TABLE 4:7	Ethnic Origins of the Political Elite				
ENGLISH	SCOTTISH	IRISH	AMERICAN	FRENCH	OTHER
12.8%	30.8%	15.4%	5.1%	30.8%	5.1%

There is almost an exact match in percentages between ethnicity and primary language with 67.5 per cent of the sample being anglophone and 32.5 per cent being francophone. Similarly, since we would expect the overwhelming majority of French Canadians to be Roman Catholic and the overwhelming majority of English-speaking Canadians to be Protestant, we were not surprised by the fact that 60 per cent of the sample were Protestant and 40 per cent were Roman Catholic. The discrepancy in percentages between ethnicity and language on the one hand and religion on the other is owing to the fact that several English-speaking members were Roman Catholic and our difficulty in ascertaining the religious affiliation of six members of our sample.

As to the occupations of the political elite, we see from data in Table 4:8 evidence of the transition from a pioneer society in which the soldier, large landholder and farmer monopolize positions of political power, to a settled, commercially oriented society in which the skills of notaries and lawyers were of considerable importance.[9] The educated middle class was further represented by journalists and businessmen.[10] Interestingly, farmers, military officers, surveyors, and seigneurs composed a relatively insignificant portion of the sample, again indicating a shift in the locus of political power.[11]

TABLE 4:8   Occupations of the Political Elite

LEGAL PROFESSION	EDITORS AND JOURNALISTS	BUSINESS-MEN	FARMERS	OTHER
56.1%	12.2%	14.6%	4.9%	12.2%

If we examine the occupational configuration of the political elite by the major constituent part of Canada the member represented, we see from data in Table 4:9 that this concentration of representatives from the commercial and professional classes was even more pronounced in Lower Canada than was the case in Upper Canada.[12]

TABLE 4:9   Occupations of the Political Elite by Upper and Lower Canada

	UPPER CANADA	LOWER CANADA
Lawyer	45%	66.7%
Journalist	10%	14.3%
Businessmen	15%	14.3%
Farmer	5%	4.8%
Other	25%	0

If we reflect upon the preceding set of data in terms of the "attitudinal prism" of the political elite, it becomes apparent that the elite can be categorized into three major groups based on socio-cultural criteria. The first group consists of native born, Roman Catholic, French Canadians representing Lower Canada. The second group consists of native born, by-and-large Protestant, English-speaking Canadians, representing Upper Canada, numerically, the smallest group. The third group consists of foreign born and raised, (largely in

the British Isles), Roman Catholic and Protestant, English-speaking
immigrants, representing both Lower and Upper Canada. These
groups, given the importance which Louis Hartz, among others, attributes to political culture as a socializing agent,[13] appear to us likely to
reflect fundamental differences in political attitudes among the elite.
While specific questions, such as the power of the party affiliation to
blunt the effects of these socio-cultural differences, must await analysis in Chapter 6, we shall now turn our attention to the second
component of the psychological environment, the actual elite images
of the Confederation question as revealed in the content analysis of
the Confederation *Debates*.

CHAPTER FIVE

Elite Images of Confederation

Following Brecher's research design for decision-making study, content analysis is employed to tap the dimension of "elite image"—the actual perceptions of the "operational environment" which the decision-making elite held. As with Brecher, our assumption is that the more the decision-making elite talk about a given factor of the operational environment, the more important they consider that dimension in arriving at their decision.[1]

Table 5:1 presents data showing the relative frequency with which elites commented on the four major components of the operational environment, Culture, Politics, Economics, and Geopolitics, in contexts both favourable and unfavourable to Confederation.

If we compute the means of the code value for each category i.e., "0"—No Mention, "3"—50.1−75 per cent, "5"—100.1 per cent and over, in terms of the percentage of columns in which these major environmental categories were discussed in the *Debates*, we find that the political area was of paramount importance, interestingly both for those arguing in favour of Confederation as well as for those arguing against it. Economic factors appear to have a distinct secondary priority in elite images, again, within both positive and negative arguments. However, in the case of images of economics, the magnitude of the difference between the positive and negative perceptions is much greater.

With regard to the areas of geopolitics and culture we find that the positive and negative images on these two dimensions are reversed. In favourable arguments, geopolitical concerns follow very closely on economic ones, while culture definitely occupies last place. In arguments unfavourable to Confederation, however, culture ranks third after economics, while negative geopolitical images are of least importance overall.

A. Images of the Internal Environment: Culture

Turning first to the area of culture, we find, looking at data in Table

TABLE 5:1 Percentage of Elite Expressing Favourable and Unfavourable Attitudes toward Confederation, Major Issue Category

	CODE	CULTURE		POLITICS		ECONOMICS		GEOPOLITICS	
		Fav	Unfav	Fav	Unfav	Fav	Unfav	Fav	Unfav
No Mention	0	48.8	58.8	39.0	46.3	39.0	61.0	46.3	58.8
1-25%	1	31.7	19.5	7.3	7.3	26.8	14.6	14.6	29.3
25.1-50%	2	12.2	14.6	7.3	9.8	22.0	9.8	22.0	12.2
50.1-75%	3	2.4	2.4	22.0	7.3	9.8	7.3	17.0	0
75.1-100%	4	4.9	4.9	9.8	4.9	0	7.3	0	0
100%+	5	0	0	14.6	24.4	2.4	0	0	0
mean of code values		.72	.75	2.0	1.9	1.1	.85	1.0	.53

TABLE 5:2 Percentage of Elite Expressing Favourable and Unfavourable Attitudes toward Confederation in the Area of Culture, by Specific Theme

	CODE	INCREASE HARMONY		PRES CULT BRITISH		PRES CULT FRENCH		CONST'T GOVT		AUTHORIT-ARIANISM	
		Fav	Unfav	Fav	Unfav	Fav	Unfav	Fav	Unfav	Fav	Unfav
No Mention	0	70.7	80.5	68.3	85.4	68.3	80.5	73.2	75.6	85.4	0
0.1-10%	1	22.0	17.1	24.4	12.2	14.6	2.4	17.1	14.6	7.3	0
10.1-20%	2	7.3	2.4	4.9	2.4	4.9	7.3	4.9	7.3	4.9	0
20.1-30%	3	0	0	2.4	0	9.8	2.4	4.9	2.4	2.4	0
30.1-40%	4	0	0	0	0	2.4	7.3	0	0	0	0
40.1%+	5	0	0	0	0	0	0	0	0	0	0
mean of code values		.36	.22	.43	.24	.63	.61	.41	.36	.24	0

5:2, that five specific themes out of eight possible, elicited significant elite commentary.

Among the cultural factors of greatest saliency, in the opinions of both proponents and opponents of Confederation, was the preservation of French culture. In looking at the actual speeches, we see that, in the main, the debate took place between French-speaking Canadians, essentially the *rouge* opposed and the *bleu* in favour. The issue turns on the degree of protection which the proposed scheme would afford French-Canadian culture as opposed to the *status quo* or some alternative course of action. Joseph Perrault eloquently puts the argument that Confederation will mean the annihilation of the French race in Canada. Further, those who favour it, specifically George Cartier, are castigated as traitors to the French-Canadian people. Perrault is warm in his praise for the existing system, with its entrenched equality, and catalogues the successes achieved under the Union: economic prosperity, an elected Upper House, the substitution of free-hold for feudal tenancy, the development of popular education, universities, and canals. Perrault is extremely mistrustful of British motives, citing past injustices visited upon the French, pointing out that reforms had to be extracted from the British, and then only when there were threatening outside forces or internal rebellion. He generally sees the proposed Confederation as an attempt to achieve representation by population, with all its attendant dire consequences for the French-speaking populace.[2] The sentiments of Perrault are reiterated by Felix Geoffrion, Henri Joly, Maurice Laframboise, and the Dorion brothers. In the same vein, the speeches of this group of dissenters contain references to Lord Durham's Report and articles from the "infamous" George Brown's *Globe*, which gave cause for concern on the issue of French-Canadian survival.

The opposite position, that the proposed scheme of Confederation would serve to enhance French-Canadian survival, is argued by a different group of French-speaking legislators. While George Cartier is the most illustrious of those taking this position, arguing that the pluralism of a federal system would be the best safeguard of French-Canadian interests,[3] it was left to others to develop this theme more fully. The contribution of A. Chartier de Lotbinière Harwood is a noteworthy example of this line of argument. Basically, Harwood places his trust in the English, pointing to the rights enjoyed in England by both Catholics and Jews and emphasizing the advantages which accrue from living in the British Empire.[4] Another point, developed by Joseph Dufresne in a speech, the bulk of which is taken up with partisan polemics against liberals like Perrault and J. B. E.

Dorion, is that Confederation, far from endangering the existence of Lower Canada, will ensure its autonomy.[5] Thus, among those members of the elite most concerned with the preservation of French culture we find diametrically opposed evaluations of the likely consequences of Confederation; on the one hand the spectre of assimilation and annihilation is raised, while on the other hand, the promise of a French-Canadian community, self-governing in those matters which concern it most, namely its culture, is held out.

The preservation of British culture did not occasion the same controversy as did the preservation of the French. The obvious reason, of course, was that the English were to be a majority in the new polity. However, where the English were to be a minority, in Lower Canada, a number of important French-Canadian leaders, Cartier, Hector Langevin, and E. P. Taché, felt it incumbent to assuage the fears of the English community that they would be unfairly dealt with by a French dominated provincial Government. One of the few English-speaking members to challenge this view was James O'Halloran of Missisquoi, who had severe misgivings about a future for the English people of Lower Canada living under francophone hegemony. O'Halloran complains about the gerrymandering of electoral boundaries to favour the French and powers of the local legislatures in the areas of constitutional change, taxation, immigration, education, and other public services. In fact, he concludes that there would be increased tension and strife between the French and English races as a result of Confederation.[6] By and large, outside of the context of the English-speaking minority in Lower Canada, the theme of preserving British culture was not dwelt upon by English-speaking contributors, with the notable exception of John Rose, who linked Confederation directly to an impending flood of British immigrants who would swell the numbers of Anglo-Saxonry in the new land.[7]

The theme of harmony between the races was certainly not a major one in the debates, however it points out an interesting juxtaposition of views. Cartier's argument that interaction between diverse ethnic groups in the context of a federal system is mutually beneficial,[8] is the most explicit statement of the positive point of view on this theme. The opposite position, is taken by Joly, who after a historical review of political confederations within his knowledge, arrives at the conclusion that federalism will increase ethnic prejudice. He mocks what he considers to be the over optimism of his adversaries by suggesting the adoption of the rainbow as the emblem of the new state.[9]

Turning to the more specific themes coded under the category of culture, constitutionalism and authoritarianism, we find that favourable arguments on the constitutionalism theme stress the advantages of British constitutional practice, with invidious comparisons made to both despotic and republican forms of government. It is noteworthy that democracy was not evaluated positively by this political elite, but rather was associated with the worst excesses of that form of government to be seen in the United States. Cartier, who was extremely critical, both of republicanism and democracy, refers to the hollowness of democracy and characterizes it as little more than mob rule.[10] Interestingly, there are no negative images of authority expressed by the elite.

Those arguments focusing on the negative aspects of constitutional government do so for the most part in two specific areas. One, and this is the case with David Reesor, is essentially a reaction to a nominated Upper House,[11] while the other, as is the case with J. H. Cameron, questions the constitutional propriety of adopting a new constitution without resort to the people by means of election.[12]

In summary, looking at elite images of Confederation in the area of culture, it is our feeling that the preservation of French culture was the only issue of major concern, and even this a concern largely restricted to the French members. For on this question a solid phalanx of detractors of Confederation, on one side, faced defenders who saw in the new political structure, greater guarantees to the integrity of French culture than provided by the status quo.

B. Images of the Internal Environment: Politics

The major area of contention in the debate over Confederation concerned the potential for this measure to resolve contemporary problems or the possible consequences resulting from the implementation of its various provisions. Depending on the speaker's point of view, the Confederation scheme was seen either as the key to a bright future of opportunity or the beginning of an endless round of constitutional bickering. Of course there were tendencies to exaggerate the possibilities of the new structure as well as opposing tendencies to prognosticate the worst. The whole tenor of the debate on this aspect was infused with the rancour of a very spirited partisanship.

The question of whether the scheme could provide a solution to the constitutional paralysis that had marked government under the Union was the most salient of all themes coded, not only within the political category, but in all other categories as well. The argument is not a simple bi-polar exchange between those who say that the new constitution will definitely break the deadlock and those who say it will not.

TABLE 5:3 Percentage of Elite Expressing Favourable and Unfavourable Attitudes toward Confederation in the Area of Politics, by Specific Theme

CODE		POLITICAL DEADLOCK		"REP BY POP"		NAT'LISM		PUBLIC OPINION		APPT OF UPPER H'SE	
		Fav	Unfav	Fav	Unfav	Fav	Unfav	Fav	Unfav	Fav	Unfav
No Mention	0	46.3	58.5	80.5	73.2	46.3	82.9	61.0	56.1	80.5	63.4
0.1-10%	1	17.1	7.3	12.3	24.4	14.6	17.1	12.2	7.3	7.3	14.6
10.1-20%	2	12.2	9.8	4.9	2.4	26.8	0	14.6	12.2	7.3	12.2
20.1-30%	3	9.8	14.6	2.4	0	9.8	0	9.8	9.8	0	7.3
30.1-40%	4	7.3	2.4	0	0	0	0	2.4	9.8	4.9	0
40%+	5	7.3	7.3	0	0	2.4	0	0	4.9	0	2.4
mean of code values		1.4	1.2	.29	.29	1.1	.17	.80	1.2	.41	.73

CODE		COMP TO LEG UNION		DIST POWER FED/LOCAL		DIST POWER PROV/PROV		TIMING		INABILITY TO AMEND	
		Fav	Unfav	Fav	Unfav	Fav	Unfav	Fav	Unfav	Fav	Unfav
No Mention	0	68.3	73.2	61.0	65.9	82.9	75.6	68.3	68.3	82.9	68.3
0.1-10%	1	29.3	17.1	22.0	14.6	9.8	12.2	14.6	14.6	12.2	17.1
10.1-20%	2	2.4	9.8	9.8	7.3	4.9	7.3	14.6	7.3	2.4	9.8
20.1-30%	3	0	0	4.9	9.8	0	2.4	0	7.3	2.4	4.9
30.1-40%	4	0	0	2.4	2.4	2.4	2.4	0	2.4	0	0
40.1%+	5	0	0	0	0	0	0	2.4	0	0	0
mean of code values		.34	.36	.66	.68	.29	.44	.56	.61	.24	.51

There were, in fact, two groups which believed that deadlock was something to be overcome and which differed from each other on how this was to be achieved. The former, arguing that Confederation provided the solution, included such spokesmen as John A. Macdonald, Joseph Cauchon, David Christie, Paul Denis, and Joseph Dufresne; while the latter included J. S. Macdonald, Matthew Crooks Cameron, A. A. Dorion, Luther Holton, Maurice Laframboise, David Reesor, and Thomas Scatcherd. In addition, there was a third view, opposed to Confederation, which stressed the value of the benefits resulting from political deadlock, where an equilibrium had been struck between the two sections of Canada. This, at least is the impression one gets from Perrault's advocacy of a continued political parity between Upper and Lower Canada.[13] A fourth opinion must be distinguished, which rejects the idea that there was any real political deadlock. In this view, supposed deadlock is nothing other than a device employed to perpetuate certain political leaders in power. Henri Joly argues specifically that no harm has resulted from a rapid turnover of ministries, and puts the case that the "true motive [for proposing Confederation] is simply a desire on their [the ministers'] parts to remain in power".[14]

One of the major issues which had produced the deadlock in the politics of the Union was the demand on the part of Upper Canadian legislators, mainly Reformers, for representation by population. It became clear that "rep by pop" would never be accepted by the representatives of Lower Canada as long as the constitution of the Union was in force, for the obvious reason that they would have found themselves in a minority position in so far as their cultural interests were concerned. Given the centrality of "rep by pop" in the historical analyses of this period, we were somewhat surprised that more of the discussion in the debates did not focus on this issue. A possible explanation for this is that arguments in favour of Confederation on the basis of "rep by pop" could easily be construed as an attack on the interests of Lower Canada which the *bleu* members of the Great Coalition had pledged to preserve. Confederation, therefore, was held up as a brilliant stroke by which Upper Canadians would get the representation due their numbers in matters which concerned them on the federal level, while Lower Canada would have a provincial government under their control to preserve the cultural values which they cherished.

Perhaps no name was more closely linked with this issue than that of George Brown, and accordingly, we would expect him to set the keynote position for those who used the "rep by pop" issue as an argument for accepting the Confederation scheme. In his address of February 8, 1865, Brown's plea for "justice" for the population of Upper Canada is counterpointed by his assurance that the Confederation scheme would increase harmony between the founding groups. The tenor of his speech is conciliatory; the issues call for concessions on both sides. Brown seems to be trying to overcome his rather strident reputation by discussing the balancing benefits to both sections.[15] His vulnerability on this point is underscored by the fact that Hope MacKenzie feels compelled to defend Brown's position against those like Christopher Dunkin, who claim that in supporting Confederation, Brown was abandoning his former principles.[16]

Those who opposed Confederation based on arguments having to do with "rep by pop" present a paradox. For among the French-Canadian antagonists of the scheme we find the argument that Confederation is merely a device to accomplish "rep by pop",[17] while among Upper Canadian detractors of the scheme, Confederation is denounced as an abdication of responsibility by those who for many years had been agitating for that principle.[18] In any event, while "rep by pop" may have been central to the bargaining process which preceded the adoption of the Quebec Resolutions, it did not occupy a particularly prominent place in the Parliamentary debates.

The spirit of nationalism has not been widely depicted as a primary motivating force behind the movement for Confederation. Yet our data reveal that among protagonists of the proposal, this theme does indeed emerge as significant. While it must be admitted that appeals to nationalism would form the basis of flowery rhetoric of the "this great country" or taking "our place among the family of nations" variety,[19] none the less speakers must have felt that such rhetoric had its purpose. Most of the commentary, however, was of a serious nature, the purpose of which was to indicate the opportunities to be gained by opening up the frontier,[20] achieving a maritime dimension,[21] the emergence of a new nationality,[22] protection against incorporation into the United States,[23] the prospects for a burgeoning economy,[24] and fostering of a more important role for Canada within the British Empire.[25] On the opposite side, there were few who spent much time criticizing Confederation from the perspective of nationalism, since their predictions of a sorry future for the scheme obviously indicated that no great national destiny was in the offing. However, the development of the new nationality was considered dangerous to some who felt that it bordered on independence and would lead to a diminishing of the ties which bound Canada to the mother country.[26]

The question of whether the plan for Confederation ought to be submitted to the people, either in the form of an election or referendum, and whether the Upper House should be elective or appointive, provided two themes on which there was widespread opposition. Significantly, many of those who favoured the overall scheme, objected strenously to these particular aspects.[27]

Supporters of the plan consistently maintained that it had to be considered as a treaty arrived at between the provinces. If such were the case, this would have been a strong argument against bringing it before the people for ratification. But it is not this legalistic kind of argument which is usually employed to forestall a referendum or election. Rather the chief argument is a political one, that in a variety of ways the people have already been consulted.[28] Further, much resort is made to historical precedent to establish that legislatures on the British model did indeed have the authority to decide significant constitutional issues.[29] Specific references to the "trustee role" of the elected member in this context were made by Alexander Campbell and John A. Macdonald.[30]

Opponents, on the other hand, argued that the people were opposed to Confederation,[31] while those who supported the overall plan, but objected to its means of implementation, argued that it would be politically unwise to embark on a new constitutional arrangement without ensuring popular support, regardless of British constitutional practice.[32]

The question of whether the Upper House should be elective or appointive provided one of the major items of disagreement between Canada and the Maritime colonies. Under the Union, a partially elected Upper House had been instituted, and this was considered a major achievement by those of the reform persuasion who now argued that because the maritimers had insisted on an appointive Upper House, consistent with their practice, Canada was to lose a hard won principle. As one might expect, it was among members of the Legislative Council where debate on this point was especially strong. A subsidiary argument by those in opposition to an appointed Upper House was the potential abuse of the power of such appointment by the government. Chief among those who argued the negative position were John Sanborn, L. A. Olivier, David Christie, David Reesor and Alexander Vidal, all members of the Legislative Council, and Thomas Scatcherd, Hope MacKenzie, and A. A. Dorion in the Legislative Assembly.

Supporters of an appointive Upper House argued on the one hand that it was a necessary concession to be made to the Maritime colonies,[33] and on the other that an appointive Upper House was in fact desirable. This latter argument is premised on the widespread fear of the excesses of the elective principle and pointed to the advantages of a "House of sober second thought", as a counterweight to the Lower House which of necessity had to react to public opinion.[34]

The next two themes, confederation as a compromise to legislative union and the distribution of power between the central government and the provincial government both deal directly with the "federal" aspects of the new constitutional plan. We note with interest that there were few real advocates of federalism as a theoretical basis of government. Supporters of the federal principle, such as John A. Macdonald and Alexander Mackenzie, saw it as a simple expedient. Both would have preferred a legislative union, but in the words of Mackenzie,

> ...in the first place...Confederation is desirable, in the second...it is attainable; and, in the third place...it is the best thing we can get, and this last is perhaps the strongest reason of all for accepting it.[35]

Federalism as a form of government is opposed on two grounds. Those who, like Christopher Dunkin, want a legislative union on the British model, are skeptical of the adaptability of federalism to this model.[36] Others, such as L. A. Olivier and Maurice Laframboise, argue that the federal principle is but a sham and that the scheme in effect provides for a surreptitious legislative union which, as Lord Durham had hoped, would spell the end of French control of their region.[37]

Closely related to the question of a federal system as opposed to a legislative union was the issue of the distribution of legislative authority which allowed local autonomy for some purposes, while at the same time ensured central direction for others. This distribution is an empirical test of the nature of the political federation. Accordingly, one finds many legislators on both sides devoting considerable attention in their speeches to this point, for this is one of the key issues which threatened the integrity of the Great Coalition. In particular, the coalition had to survive the apparent contradiction of J. A. Macdonald assuring the House that the central government would be stronger than that provided for in the American constitution,[38] and Hector Langevin and George Cartier reassuring their compatriots that they would be better protected under the proposed system than they were under the Union.[39]

The *rouge* opposition was not to let this ambivalence pass without comment. The thrust of their attack was against their *bleu* countrymen, whom they accused of self interest bordering on treason. A. A. Dorion takes issue with the distribution of power, noting that as a result of Confederation, French Canadians would be unable to control their destinies in matters touching on marriage legislation, divorce, and the union of civil and canon law, among other issues in the legal domain. He is also not satisfied with answers he had received as to who would adjudicate disputes between central and provincial jurisdictions.[40] His brother, J. B. E. Dorion, takes particular issue with the 51st resolution, which gives the power of veto to the central government and scoffs at the claim that it would be rarely used.[41] This tack is followed by other *rouges* such as Laframboise and Geoffrion.

No one could have disagreed more with this position than James O'Halloran, who argues that Confederation does indeed give the French Canadians the power to determine a wide range of matters in Lower Canada, so much so, that the English-speaking minority within the French minority would be entirely within the power of the French.[42] Thus with the exception of the *bleus*, almost no one sees Confederation as failing to lean one way or the other in the direction of either centralism or localism.

The issue of the distribution of power between the provinces touched mainly on the relative power position of Canada in relation to the Maritime colonies in the new constitutional structure. A number of legislators opposed Confederation on the grounds that too much had been conceded to the Maritimes. In addition to the question of the elected vs appointive Upper House, which we have already discussed, and the apportionment of debt and taxation and the building of the Intercolonial Railway, which we will discuss in their proper context under Economics, the political issue involved in the Canadian -Maritime controversy turned on the number of seats to be allotted to the various components parts of the new Confederation.

James Currie argues that in the deliberations leading up to the adoption of the Quebec Resolutions, the Canadian provinces were not given votes proportionate to their population. Thus, in matters of numbers in the new Parliament, Canada came up short. With specific reference to the Legislative Council, Currie argues as follows:

> ... it was proposed to give Upper Canada and Lower Canada twenty-four members each, and to the Lower Provinces twenty-eight. That is, the 780,000 souls of the Lower Provinces would have four members more than Upper Canada with its million and a half.[43]

Thus while Confederation would recognize the superior population of Upper Canada vis-à-vis Lower Canada, it would not recognize the superiority in numbers of that section to the Maritime colonies. Benjamin Seymour and A. A. Dorion likewise characterize the scheme as a sell out—to the Maritime provinces.[44]

In answering these arguments that Canada has yielded too much, Alexander Campbell takes the position of the Maritimes and argues that the discrepancies in power and numbers between the two regions lead those in the Maritimes to believe "that everything which they desire for themselves will be trampled under foot".[45] Thus the argument is made, in effect, that as all sides are complaining, the Confederation proposals must have been a good compromise. In this same vein, Hope MacKenzie points out that compromise is always difficult to reach, and that all had to make concessions in order to "unite sectional interests of the provinces and to further something like a nationality for the country".[46]

The final two issues considered under the rubric of politics concerned two questions which at times were intertwined; one being the argument as to whether Confederation had to be consummated with some speed, and the second, whether or not legislators would be free to offer amendments to the proposals.

James Currie is again found in the ranks of the opposition, arguing that

> In a matter of this momentous importance, upon which the well-being of millions in the future might so much depend, he sincerely trusted the country would not be hurried, but that full time for discussion would be given to enable it to arrive at a safe verdict.[47]

David Reesor argues along the same line that "Constitutions are not usually made in a day, and that they should not be passed in a week; they are matters of too grave a character".[48] Alexander Vidal and Benjamin Seymour also counsel delay.[49]

As with the question of the distribution of power between the provinces, Alexander Campbell, Commissioner of Crown Lands, delivers the government's rebuttal in the Legislative Council. He states that there is no purpose to be served by delay, in that in British constitutional practice, there is no practical way to consult the people.[50] In the Assembly, a number of key members of the government responded in the same way to the calls for delay.[51] It was apparent that the government was very concerned with the possible consequences of procrastination and was anxious to avoid any deferral of the issue. Among those who argued for delay, we do find some overlapping of anti- and pro-Confederation members, for while those opposed to Confederation used the timing issue as simply one more instrument to attack the scheme,[52] some pro-Confederationists exhibited genuine concern that the proposal would not achieve its best results if it were enacted with too much haste.[53]

Those who favoured amendments to the proposals before Parliament argued that the legislative body should have the right to amend measures before it for approval. But the government argued that amendment is only a right in regard to internal legislation, not when a treaty is up for ratification. On this point government spokesmen argued that the measure before the House was indeed a treaty, a pact arrived at between the Maritime colonies and Canada.

The primary issue over which the question of amendment arose was the need for some form of popular ratification. In the Council such an amendment is put forward by James Currie to the effect that the Council "is unwilling to assume the responsibility of assenting to a measure involving so many important considerations, without a further manifestation of public will than has yet been declared".[54] A similar amendment was introduced in the Assembly by J. H. Cameron after that body voted in favour of the proposals.[55]

The government laboured to keep the principle of amendment from gaining legitimacy. In the Council, Alexander Campbell used the argument that any amendment would be considered as a vote of no confidence, which would endanger acceptance of the proposals in the Maritimes.[56] John A. Macdonald likens the proposals to a treaty to which no important change can be made. He further argues that to amend the proposals means that "every one of the colonies will feel itself absolved from the implied obligation to deal with it as a Treaty", with the result that any alteration of the agreement implies complete renegotiation.[57] D'Arcy McGee asserts the legal power of the Assembly to make treaties by the right of coaction and he then goes on to expand Macdonald's argument as to the necessity of a treaty being unalterable.[58] The opposite position rests on the belief as expressed by David Reesor, "that we have been elected to this Legislature with a view to perfect as far as possible every scheme or proposition that may properly come before it".[59]

Examining elite attitudes toward Confederation in the sphere of politics, it is possible to view them in terms of two general categories: responsible government and integration.

If the principal issue behind political deadlock in the Union was representation by population, the government thought that it had solved that problem by giving to Upper Canada the power due to it as a majority, while ensuring minority rights, both political and religious. The government did not argue that the people should not be consulted at all, but that there had been adequate consultation along the lines of responsible government on the Westminster model. The employment of referenda is generally inimical to that model. The problem of responsible government also arises when the makeup of the Upper House is discussed. The government rejects the argument for popular control and maintains, not only that the Upper House will be constituted according to the principle of provincial representation, but will provide a vehicle for sober second thoughts. Finally, the purposes behind amendment are criticized not simply on treaty grounds, but once again because a short delay will not be sufficient to consult the people, and in any case, no new consultation is required.

The opposition, on the other hand, insofar as it constitutes a bloc of opinion, rejects the Confederation solution, maintaining that the demand for representation based on population can best be ensured by a legislative union—an opinion obviously confined to the Upper Canada opposition—and that minority rights are not safeguarded, whether it be the rights of the Lower Canadian French Catholic population or, the minority in a minority, the Lower Canadian English Protestant population. The opposition demands an appeal to the people, perhaps as a delaying tactic, but ideologically because of a commitment to popular sovereignty. Amendment was the main device used in order to allow time for popular consultation. The same commitment accounts for the advocacy of an elective Upper House responsible to and removeable by the electorate.

In regard to the second category of arguments, those bearing on political integration, the differences between government and opposition are equally trenchant.

In order to overcome the shortcomings of the Union, the government supported a national scheme. The strength of its position was that Confederation clearly would be more conducive to the development of a political nationality than the Union and that a big Canada afforded the possibility of national greatness not possible with a little Canada. They could also look to the benefits promised by western expansion. While admitting some weaknesses existed in the details of the scheme, the government argued that the scheme must be examined as a whole.

As to the federal system itself, the government argued that the distribution of powers between federal government and provincial governments struck a nice balance between the need for central direction and the desire for local autonomy. The government spokesmen admitted that the Maritime provinces had been given more power, particularly in the Upper House, than their numbers warranted, but this was a compromise necessary if there was to be an agreement at all. Since Confederation was a treaty, the government held that no amendments could be made to it. It had to be accepted or rejected *in toto*. Any delay would require the complete renegotiation of the pact with results which no one could foresee.

The opposition did not really attack the idea of nationalism. Its criticisms aimed at the details of the system rather than the system as a whole. Opposition members are mistrustful of the project, attributing interested motives to its proponents (the maintenance of themselves in office). Beyond this, the opponents fasten on a number of specific aspects. Some of them thought that government had exceeded its authority in putting forth proposals for a federation of all the British North American colonies, whereas its mandate had been to resolve the differences between the two Canadas, that is by establishing a legislative union. The distribution of powers between the federal government and the provinces was criticized, particularly by French Canadians, as failing to protect French-Canadian cultural interests by assigning to them legal control over certain matters. The opposition was vehement in denouncing the "sellout" to the Maritime colonies which gave them a power incommensurate with their population. Finally, the opposition did not agree that any delay would be disastrous and argued, on the contrary, that great schemes of government should not be hastily accepted.

Thus there was no common agreement between government and opposition either on the need for a new scheme of government, nor, if that need were granted, on the structure which was proposed to it, nor on the details of the plan and its implementation.

C. Images of the Internal Environment: Economics

Proponents of Confederation have traditionally been credited with seeking to establish an alternative economic system to the one which had been overturned in the 1840s by the end of mercantilism and the advent of free trade in England. The anticipated abrogation of the Reciprocity Treaty of 1854 which had opened the American market to Canadian trade prompted the search for a replacement for that system.

Data in Table 5:4 appear to confirm that the political elite of the 1860s indeed offered economic inducements as arguments for the proposed union. Opponents of the scheme, on the other hand, while

TABLE 5:4   Percentage of Elite Expressing Favourable and Unfavourable Attitudes toward Confederation in the Area of Economics, by Specific Theme

	CODE	TRADE AND COMMERCE		GENERAL PROSPERITY		RAILWAYS		COSTS OF CONFEDERATION	
		Fav	Unfav	Fav	Unfav	Fav	Unfav	Fav	Unfav
No Mention	0	51.2	78.0	53.7	78.0	61.0	73.2	53.7	61.0
0.1-10%	1	22.0	12.2	26.8	19.5	31.7	9.8	26.8	7.3
10.1-20%	2	17.1	7.3	12.2	2.4	7.3	12.2	7.3	9.8
20.1-30%	3	4.9	2.4	4.9	0	0	0	9.8	9.8
30.1-40%	4	2.4	0	2.4	0	0	2.4	0	4.9
40% +	5	2.4	0	0	0	0	2.4	2.4	7.3
mean of code values		.92	.34	.75	.24	.46	.56	.83	1.1

unconvinced that major economic benefits were likely to ensue, were more concerned with the likely costs which would be the legacy of Confederation, particularly the building of the Intercolonial Railway.

Alexander Galt, Minister of Finance, presents the government's case in favour of Confederation based on increased trade and commerce and an enhanced general prosperity. His arguments stress the advantages to be gained from having an economic base which would not depend on one industry, and accordingly points out the diversity of riches in the proposed union. Furthermore, he demonstrates the benefits, in terms of a healthy trading picture, which the Maritimes would bring into Confederation.[60] Because of the Maritimes, Canada has the potential of becoming a great seafaring power. Galt finds another major reason for Confederation in the argument that it will break down the tariff barriers that have contributed to the insignificant level of trade between Canada and the Maritime colonies "and the opening up of the markets of all the provinces to the different industries of each".[61] He specifically points to Confederation as providing alternative markets to those in the United States which appear threatened by the end of reciprocity. According to Galt, Canadians should "seek by free trade with our fellow colonists for a continued and uninterrupted commerce which will not be liable to be disturbed at the capricious will of any foreign country".[62]

William McGiverin and A. Chartier Lotbinière Harwood echo Galt's economic optimism. Fearing the consequences of American economic policies on Canada, McGiverin sees Confederation as a solution. "By union with the Lower Provinces, it is evident that we will be enabled to increase our trade to the amount of five or six millions of dollars, which is of itself a very strong inducement, aside from other considerations that I have alluded to."[63] Harwood stresses the commercial advantages of union, pointing to the considerable resources to be gained in fish, timber, and coal.[64]

These economic arguments are challenged by a number of speakers. J. B. E. Dorion ridicules the idea that the Maritime colonies provide a lucrative trading partner for Canada in that products produced there tend to be similar to those produced in Canada. As put by Dorion, "What trade could there be between two farmers who produced nothing but oats? . . . They might stand and stare at each other with their oats before them, without ever being able to trade together; they would require a third person—a purchaser".[65] He goes on to compare the economic uniformity of the two regions with the United States and its climatic diversity, which brings about complementary needs. In any case, argues Dorion, any possible trading advantages would be attainable without the necessity of political unification. As evidence, he points to the Reciprocity Treaty between Canada and the United States and offers as an alternative to Confederation a simple system of free trade between the colonies.[66]

Arguing along a different line, M. C. Cameron disputes the connection between low tariffs and the Reciprocity Treaty on the one hand, with Upper Canadian economic prosperity on the other. Arguing that Upper Canada was prosperous prior to lower tariffs and Reciprocity, he downplays the possible repercussions of an American protectionist policy, stating, "I have yet to see, if the reciprocity treaty is put an end to and if the bonding system is discontinued, that we would be unable to find means by which the energies of this country would find development".[67]

It is obvious from the arguments both of those stressing the economic advantages of Confederation, as well as those who were skeptical of any appreciable increase in economic advantage flowing from the scheme, that general prosperity was in fact measured largely in terms of levels of trade. Concomitant with the predictions of a growing trade between Canada and the Maritime provinces was the necessity of the speedy completion of the Intercolonial Railway to facilitate this commercial intercourse. In addition, the railway was looked upon by many advocates of Confederation as a necessary component of the Canadian defence system against a possible American attack.

Chief spokesmen arguing in favour of Confederation on the basis of the construction of the Intercolonial Railway were John Ross, J. H. Cameron, John Rose, Frederick Haultain, and Alexander Mackenzie. Ross' argument is the fullest. Quoting from the Durham Report, Ross argues that the Intercolonial is necessary in order to ensure uninterrupted trade for Canada. Further, he assails the notion that the railway is unpopular, stating: "I feel morally certain that if the subject were fairly discussed in every town in Upper Canada, nine-tenths of the people would go heartily for it. Indeed, the railway is absolutely necessary and we cannot do without it".[68] He goes on to argue that opponents have exaggerated the costs and that it is of equal benefit to Canada and the Maritimes. His final argument in favour of the Intercolonial rests on its necessity in the event that reciprocity with the United States is ended.

J. H. Cameron presents the military argument that the Intercolonial is necessary for Canadian defence. Cameron is willing to incur the debt involved in the building of the road in order to avoid "the liability we now labour under, of having our connection with Great Britain cut off".[69] John Rose defends the railway against the charge leveled by A. A. Dorion, "that the whole arrangement was merely a nicely planned scheme for the benefit of the Grand Trunk Railway".[70] Quoting Lord Derby, Rose contends that the railway is necessary for the defence of the provinces.[71]

Both Frederick Haultain and Alexander Mackenzie stress the political rather than the economic or military benefits of the Intercolonial. Haultain specifically acknowledges the short run expense and both the commercial and military limitations of the road. Nevertheless, he sees it as essential for purposes of political integration.[72] Alexander Mackenzie argues likewise, stating "without the road there can be no union of the provinces".[73]

Opponents, on the other hand, saw in the railway a major reason for opposition toward Confederation. They questioned its cost, especially since they felt that on both economic and military grounds, it made little sense. But beyond this, the entire scheme of Confederation was depicted as nothing more than a machination to further the interest of the Grand Trunk Railway.

This latter theme is developed most fully by A. A. Dorion, who claims that after an earlier scheme to gain approval for the building of the Intercolonial Railway had failed, "the Confederation of all the British North American Provinces naturally suggested itself to the Grand Trunk officials as the surest means of bringing with it the construction of the Intercolonial Railway".[74] He also scoffs at the notion that the railway will be useful for defence and generally questions an undertaking which has no firm cost attached to it.[75]

Thomas Scatcherd is another who sees "the hand of the Grand Trunk in this Confederation scheme".[76] In addition, he is concerned not only with the cost of construction, estimated at twenty million dollars, but with the continuing costs of operation as well. Scatcherd alleges, "this road will have to be run at the expense of this province, and not only that, but it will be a piece of corruption from the time of the turning of the first shovelful of earth".[77] Furthermore, he claims that the money, to his mind wasted on this unprofitable railway, could be spent to better advantage in the opening up of the northwest.[78]

James Currie complains not only of the costs of the Intercolonial, but also about the lack of information regarding the specific route of the railway.[79] He goes on to remind the members of the Council of the unsavoury history of the Grand Trunk and its finances and suggests that it is no accident that officials of the Grand Trunk are to a man supporters of Confederation.[80] David Reesor assails the unequal distribution of costs involved in building the railway, claiming that the Upper Canadians will have to pay the lion's share of a railway whose

benefits are mainly for the Maritime colonies. He further asserts that
the present conditions of building the railway are decidedly less favourable to Upper Canada than were the conditions discussed two
years previously, and even those conditions, he maintains, would have
cost the government its office if any election had been fought on
them.[81]

M. C. Cameron adds another dimension to the debate. In addition
to opposing the Intercolonial on financial grounds, Cameron mounts a
personal attack on George Brown for his latter day conversion from a
policy of financial retrenchment to one of lavish expenditure. Quoting
extensively from *Globe* articles which had earlier denounced the Intercolonial, Cameron asks pointedly, "Is the only change that has taken
place the elevation of the editor to a seat at the Executive Council
Board?"[82]

With regard to the Intercolonial Railway, the most pervasive objection was the enormous burden of the cost to be assigned to the
Province of Canada, while at the same time the benefits were considered to be marginal at best. While the Intercolonial furnished one
concrete financial objection to Confederation, it was by no means the
only one, as detractors also questioned the financial soundness of the
entire arrangement.

Charged with presenting the government's position on the distribution of costs in the new Confederation is Minister of Finance, Alexander Galt, who demonstrates that the costs are assigned equitably
among the partners. One of the bases on which he makes this claim
has to do with the nature of the public debts incurred by the various
provinces, which he argues are alike in that they have been the result
of expenditures on means of transportation and communication towards the end of increasing trade. These works have between them,
resulted in a network which shows the naturalness of the proposed
union.[83] After reviewing the relative debt positions of the Maritime
provinces as well as that of Canada, Galt concludes that the scheme
is financially sound and that Canadian taxpayers would not be assuming obligations contracted by others.[84] Furthermore, with regard
to the financial resources of the lower provinces, Galt emphasizes
that they "have been and are now in a position to meet, from their
taxation, all their expenses and cannot be regarded as bringing any
burthen to the people of Canada".[85]

Hector Langevin, in addition to repeating some of Galt's justifica-
tions of Confederation for the benefit of the French members, dismisses arguments against Confederation based on excessive cost by
warning the legislature that if the alternative to Confederation should

be annexation to the United States, Canada would be subject to a debt burden of six times greater magnitude per head.[86] He further points out that the specific exemption given to New Brunswick with respect to the collection of export duty on timber was necessary since this was a crucial revenue for that province to defray its local expenses. Without this concession there could be no union.[87] He also attempts to allay the fears that there would be a resort to direct taxation as a consequence of Confederation and accuses A. A. Dorion of "attempting to trade on popular prejudice" especially in order to alarm the people of Lower Canada.[88] On the contrary, Langevin asserts after outlining the other revenues available to Lower Canada, that "the people will see that there is no danger of direct taxation with the surplus revenue we shall have. Direct taxation must be resorted to if Lower Canada should give way to extravagance and spend more than her means, but not otherwise".[89]

Alexander Mackenzie meets the concern that there will be increased costs attendant on the new form of government claiming that "I believe we shall be able to govern as cheaply united as we now do separately".[90] His brother Hope MacKenzie defends the basis on which public debt is allocated, to wit—population, and dismisses the view that revenue would be a fairer test of ability to pay, given the differing means of raising revenues in the various provinces. Overall, he concludes "that every one of the five provinces has had its interests well consulted in this scheme, and that it is so well balanced throughout in reference to those interests, that there is very little to complain of".[91] In the same vein, Paul Denis maintains that just as those such as A. A. Dorion criticize Confederation as detrimental to the financial interests of Canada, there are those in the Maritimes who argue that it portends financial ruin for them.[92]

Among the leading critics of the financial provisions of the new constitutional scheme were the Dorion brothers. A. A. Dorion is especially outraged at the apparent benefits which will accrue to the lower provinces at the expense of Canada and characterizes New Brunswick and Nova Scotia as the "favoured children of the Confederation".[93] Chief among these benefits is the right given to New Brunswick to levy export duties on lumber. Also objectionable to Dorion are the purchase of the mineral lands of Newfoundland and the building of the Intercolonial Railway.[94] Dorion believes that projected debt of twenty-five dollars per head is excessive compared to the per capita debt of a much wealthier Imperial England.[95]

J. B. E. Dorion envisions Confederation as entailing great costs which would necessitate direct taxation. Local parliaments would be-

come in Dorion's estimation no more than "taxing machines".[96] His
general assault on the costs of Confederation is well expressed when
he says, "I am opposed to the scheme of Confederation, because it is
most unjustly proposed to enrich the Lower Provinces with annuities
and donations, to persuade and induce them to enter into a union
which will be injurious to all the contracting parties".[97] Secondly, he
is critical of the manner in which the public debts of the provinces
have been apportioned. Finally, he finds the premium offered to New
Brunswick to be extraordinary.[98]

Thomas Scatcherd decries the fact that from the first days of Confederation the new government will be called upon to pay large sums
for interest on the public debt and subsidies to the various provinces.[99] This outlay, coupled with loss of revenue from customs, will
yield a bleak financial picture. On the basis of a viewpoint founded
essentially on the paramount interest of Upper Canada, Scatcherd
concludes, after a spirited debate with George Brown, that in his
opinion there is little benefit for Upper Canada in the scheme, in that
the people of Upper Canada will be saddled with the larger portion of
the expense.[100]

In the Legislative Council, James Currie expresses his strong opposition to the financial arrangements, claiming that "Confederation
means more debt, more taxation, and a worse public credit".[101]

In the speeches which concern the economic issues behind Confederation, the manner in which proponents and opponents present their
arguments are strikingly dissimilar. The spokesmen for the government use quite general reasons to show why Confederation is desirable, offering the vista of expanded trade, increased prosperity and
profits under the new system. The critics, on the other hand, employ
detailed information, attack specific provisions, and assume the hard
nosed cost-accountancy approach to the proposals. They question the
commercial benefits; they closely scrutinize the railroad; they raise
tough questions about the overall costs.

The government speakers state that Confederation will allow Canada to adjust to the replacement of the mercantilist system by Great
Britain for one of free trade, by establishing an internal market en-
compassing all the provinces. Opponents respond that one does not
need Confederation in order to have better trade relations either with
the Maritimes or with the United States. The Intercolonial Railway is
supported by the advocates for both economic and military reasons.
The economic reasons are linked with the need to have a transportation network with the Maritimes. The military argument is that without a railway, there could be no logistic support for a defence force

poised on the border with the truculent Yankees. The opponents claim that the railway is not to further Confederation, but Confederation is a scheme for the betterment of the shareholders of the Grand Trunk. They go on to point out the hollowness of the military argument and insist that the considerable outlay for the railway could be more profitably utilized for western expansion. Then it is noted that the members have been informed neither of the route of the proposed road nor of the estimated costs of the line. The peoples of Canada are to be burdened with debt in order to bring development to the Maritimes.

Galt tried to persuade the House that the costs of Confederation were in fact equitably distributed. The concessions made to New Brunswick were necessary and fair. On the contrary, the critics say that favouritism has been shown to the Maritimes. Furthermore, direct taxation will be inevitable since the costs of the new system cannot be alleviated by other means.

D. Images of the External Environment

The external context in which the Confederation debates took place made geopolitical factors of some consequence in the considerations of many of the legislators. Thus the perceived hostility of the United States, as exemplified by the *Trent* Affair, the Alabama claims, border incidents, and New York editorialists promoting northern expansion, formed the backdrop for speeches which concentrated on defence policy, possible annexation to the United States, need for Canadian western development and Canada's place within the British Imperial defence system. As data in Table 5:5 indicate, all these themes were used more extensively to promote Confederation than they were to defeat it.

This issue on which greatest debate took place was that of Canadian defence policy. The position of the government on defence was presented by D'Arcy McGee. Arguing that Canada is "compelled, by warning voices from within and without, to make a change", McGee emphasizes two points: 1) that Canada must become more responsible for her own defence, and 2) that the United States has given a number of indications that this defence may well be necessary. He points particularly to the enormous increase in the armed forces of the United States, which he catalogues in terms of manpower and weaponry.[102] McGee feels that the worst result of the increase in armaments in the United States has been the change in attitude there from a peaceful demeanour to one that glorifies violence.[103] Citing the

TABLE 5:5 Percentage of Elite Expressing Favourable and Unfavourable Attitudes toward Confederation in the Area of Geopolitics, by Specific Theme

	CODE	DEFENCE POLICY		FEAR OF ANNEXATION		CANADIAN WESTERN DEVELOPMENT		STRENGTHEN IMPERIAL CONNECTION	
		Fav	Unfav	Fav	Unfav	Fav	Unfav	Fav	Unfav
No Mention	0	51.2	63.4	56.1	78.0	80.5	25.4	53.7	87.8
0.1-10%	1	14.6	9.8	24.4	19.5	12.2	12.2	17.1	4.9
10.1-20%	2	24.4	19.5	12.2	2.4	4.9	2.4	19.5	7.3
20.1-30%	3	4.9	7.3	7.3	0	2.4	0	4.9	0
30.1-40%	4	4.9	0	0	0	0	0	4.9	0
40.1% +	5	0	0	0	0	0	0	0	0
mean of code values		.97	.70	.70	.24	.29	.17	.90	.19

adage that "no nation ever had the power of conquest that did not use it, or abuse it, at the very first favourable opportunity", McGee draws to the attention of the legislators the need, through Confederation, to protect the British flag in North America.[104]

John Rose adds to the argument the British dimension when he asserts that the question of how or even whether to defend British North America has become a matter of public debate in Britain.[105] In this context, he maintains that Confederation will serve as a signal to Britain that Canada is willing, with Britain's help, to defend herself and urges that Confederation be undertaken at the earliest moment to give such assurance.[106] Moreover, he stresses the military advantages to be attained by the overall direction of any defence posture or war effort by a central government.[107] Harwood similarly indicates that to unite would prove to England "that we intend to organize a system so as to do our part in the hour of danger",[108] and cites from the pages of history examples to demonstrate the strength of federation. J. H. Cameron also reiterates the need to prepare for war so as to avoid it and to demonstrate to England that a united Canada will be worthy of her military support.[109]

In the Council, Premier Taché sees Canada facing the "twofold danger of being dragged violently into the American Union, and in the next place, as we stood on an inclined plane, of slipping down gradually, and without our being aware of it, into the vortex below".[110] He stresses the military disadvantages of a possible winter campaign, where Canada would be cut off from supplies and British support.[111] For Taché, Confederation will reinforce the capacity to resist.

These propositions were controverted by opponents of Confederation. Benjamin Seymour maintains that the resources available for defence would not be that much greater after Confederation than before, particularly in view of the stated unwillingness of the Maritime provinces to support increased expenditures for defence.[112]

Luther Holton, while acknowledging that defence is necessary, warns that the enthusiasm on this subject on the part of proponents of Confederation would lead to costly expenditures, perhaps even a standing army, which would create financial ruin and would bring about the very demise of the country that this defence effort was meant to forestall.[113]

J. B. E. Dorion attacks the notion that Confederation will aid in the defence of the country on several counts. For one, he discounts the purported usefulness of the Intercolonial Railway as a military resource, as he questions its proximity to the American border and

therefore its vulnerability to enemy attack. Further, he questions the
number of troops which it would take to keep it serviceable.[114] A
second ground of criticism of the defence implications of Confederation involves costs. For Dorion says that Canadians might become
burdened by the costs engendered by a war between England and the
United States, "a war in which they could neither say anything to
avoid, nor in its progress take any other part than that of shedding
their blood and paying their money".[115] Furthermore, he cautions that
England, given its past record in the Crimean War, is unlikely to be
able to provide the kind of backing so optimistically predicted by
speakers such as John Rose and J. H. Cameron.[116] He goes on to
stress the strength of the United States and advises his fellow legislators that any future conflict with the United States will not be like
that of 1812, in that the people of Lower Canada could not be
expected to fight as they had in that conflict.[117]

A. A. Dorion likewise questions the logic underlying the strength
in union argument, asserting that two plus two equals four, not five.
Indeed, according to Dorion, Canada would add a greater frontier to
defend without adding as large a proportional number of people to
defend it.[118] He agrees with others that the expense to be undertaken
would be intolerable, and would be in the main for the defence of the
Lower Provinces.[119] His overall counsel, given his appraisal of defence
responsibility and capability in the face of American power, is stated
as follows: "the best thing that Canada can do is to keep quiet and to
give no cause for war".[120]

Closely related to the defence theme is that of possible annexation
to the United States. In this regard, Taché warns that unless measures
are taken to bolster the defence of Canada, it shall find itself faced
with the unhappy alternatives of forcible subjugation or gradual assimilation into the American republic. For Taché,

> ... if we do not cultivate with our sister provinces—the Maritime Provinces—
> a close commercial, political, and social intercourse, ... we run a great dan-
> ger. We are in our present position, small isolated bodies, and it may
> probably be with us, as in the physical world, where a large body attracts to
> itself the smaller bodies within the sphere of its influence. If we do not make
> those alliances with the Lower Provinces ... we shall little by little lose some
> of those principles we now esteem so much; we shall lose little by little our
> attachment to the Mother Country ... and we shall become—you may de-
> pend upon it, hon. gentlemen—more and more democratised before we are
> aware of it.[121]

In the assembly, George Cartier introduces the same point, claiming that:

> The matter resolved itself into this; either we must obtain British North American Confederation or be absorbed in an American Confederation.[122]

Cartier goes on to accuse the *rouge* opposition of conspiring to defeat British North American Confederation in order to permit the accomplishment of their own goal, which he claims is annexation of Lower Canada to the American republic.[123]

D'Arcy McGee points to the great risks involved in rejecting Confederation. For McGee, high among those risks is that of "being swallowed up by the spirit of universal democracy that prevails in the United States".[124] Maintaining that universal democracy in the American continent is as unacceptable as universal monarchy in Europe, McGee offers Confederation as a bulwark against the democratic tide. If Confederation is not achieved reasons McGee, "the Lower Provinces—the smaller fragments—will be 'gobbled up' first, and we will come in afterwards by way of dessert".[125]

J. B. E. Dorion attempts to turn the annexation argument against the spokesmen favouring Confederation. First he emphasizes that he is not advocating annexation nor claiming that the people want annexation. Rather, he states, that the social and economic conditions in Canada favour a democratic rather than a monarchical form of government, monarchy entailing for Dorion "extravagance, ruin, and anarchy".[126] He praises the American constitution, and predicts that if Canada adopts the plan of Confederation presented in the Quebec Resolutions, it will be the surest means of bringing about annexation as it will "create serious discontent, and a constant conflict between us and our neighbours".[127] Joseph Perrault in a speech which complements Dorion's, avers that as the Confederation scheme threatens the continuation of the French Canadian race, in the conflict which he sees likely between England and the United States, the French Canadians will opt for supporting the latter.[128]

While both supporters and opponents of Confederation were concerned with the "pull" of America drawing Canada into its sphere, in particular, supporters saw Confederation as strengthening the ties which bound Canada to the Mother Country. Speaking in this vein we find Alexander Campbell who chastizes his opponents for refusing to join in an enterprise that would bring "a closer connection with the Mother Country and a better means of perpetuating British institutions on this continent".[129] He goes on to argue that the relationship with Britain cannot be maintained without Confederation, which among other things will indicate to skeptics in the Mother Country that Canada is willing to do her part to maintain the integrity of the Empire.[130]

Alexander Morris answers the assertions of detractors of Confederation that it will weaken imperial ties. He sketches the development of British colonial policy since Lord Durham's day, the encouragement of the development of a Canadian nationality, and thinks that the line that binds Canada to Britain will be strengthened by the proposed union, in which Canadians will be proud to maintain that they are British subjects.[131]

Colonel Frederick Haultain points out that the opposition is trying to foster the impression that Britain is not particularly interested in maintaining its connection with Canada and dismisses the references alluded to by spokesmen such as Dunkin as minority reflections of the Manchester School persuasion.[132] He replies to critics by citing various Lords of the realm to the effect that England is happy with Confederation and feels it will cement the colonial relationship.[133] Along the same line, J. H. Cameron refutes the Manchester economists with statistical evidence from which he concludes that "the colonies are of much more value to the Mother Country than is generally supposed, and much more than the school of politicians to which I have referred would have people believe".[134] Cameron goes back to his earlier position on defence that Canada must demonstrate to England by financial sacrifice, that it is willing to defend itself.[135]

Opponents of Confederation attempted to characterize the scheme as laying the groundwork for a deterioration in relations with Britain and even worse, creating the conditions for the eventual severing of the imperial link. Christopher Dunkin leans heavily on the argument that Confederation deflects the Province of Canada from its true need which is to cultivate the relationship with Britain, rather than to seek out an alliance of dubious advantage with the Lower Provinces.[136]

M. C. Cameron fears that Confederation may lead to independence and counsels rejection on the grounds that "we can never be so great in any way as we can by remaining a dependency of the British Crown".[137] Benjamin Seymour questions the mechanisms whereby Confederation will supposedly strengthen the connection with Britain. If that were the case, why he asks is it that the financial reformers who want to separate the colonies from Great Britain all advocate "this measure in the warmest possible manner?"[138] For Seymour, talk of Confederation, far from strengthening the imperial connection, will result in its termination.

While concern for maintaining the British connection was a reflection of the desire to keep the links with the past, the northwest territories provided opportunities for vistas of a continental dream.[139] In this vein, William McGiverin insists that he would not cast his vote in favour of Confederation if it did not give promise of pursuing vigorously the development of western lands.[140] He alludes to the riches of these territories and cites figures of the wealth that has been attained in the American western hinterland. He regrets that Canadians have not taken advantage of the mineral wealth, agricultural promise, and economic opportunities that await them by opening up the northwest.[141]

Alexander Mackenzie links the development of the northwest, entailed in Confederation, with future national growth through a "prodigious increase in our population and an immense development of strength and power".[142] Alexander Morris similarly refers to the great promise of the northwest and warns that the failure to achieve Confederation will lead to the inevitable result "that that great section of territory will be taken possession of by the citizens of the neighbouring states".[143] He goes on to point out that the Red River settlement forms the basis of a future province which has remarkably fertile soil and could serve as a base of agricultural strength.[144]

The opponents to Confederation also saw the promise of western development, but perceived Confederation as an impediment to this development since resources would be diverted towards less valuable projects necessary to cement relations with the Lower Provinces.

Thomas Scatcherd holds that as the Intercolonial Railway is a part of the constitution it must therefore be completed. The opening of the west, however, receives no such priority and remains dependent on funds becoming available. Arguing from an Upper Canadian position that it is "most important for the interest of this country that that territory should be opened up to settlement", Scatcherd opposes Confederation.[145] M. C. Cameron and Arthur Rankin both complain that the development of the west is not guaranteed by the new constitution. However, while Rankin, a supporter of Confederation, is merely concerned, Cameron feels that it is a major objection to the adoption of the scheme.[146] Christopher Dunkin similarly compares the absolute commitment to the Intercolonial Railway with the qualified endorsement of the development of the north-west, contingent upon available finances.[147]

Four questions were posed in regard to the geopolitical dimension
of Confederation. First, will Confederation make the country militar-
ily stronger or not? Second, will Confederation end the annexationist
danger or hasten it? Third, will the scheme strengthen or weaken the
imperial bond? Fourth, will the scheme favour western expansion or
not?

In answer to the first question, the proponents argue that the union
of the provinces will increase the strength now possessed by the
several provinces. The opponents, on the other hand, say that the
resources at the disposal of the united provinces will be no greater
and that consequently, their strength will remain the same. In answer
to the second question, the proponents warn that Canada is in danger
of being drawn into the American field of force, while the opponents
claim that Confederation will bring annexation closer through increased taxation, by provoking the Americans, and by alienating the
French Canadians. As to the third question, proponents point out that
Great Britain supports the scheme as is clear from the declarations of
notable statesmen and that the bond will be preserved. The opponents
say that English politicians indeed support Confederation, but precisely because they wish to sever the bond. Furthermore, ending the
status of a dependency will eventually lead to full independence.
Finally, supporters of Confederation enumerate the wealth of the west
and Confederation as a means to extending Canada westward. The
opponents say that Confederation is an impediment to western development, for the building of the Intercolonial Railway precludes in-
vestment needed for expansion to the west.

To sum up, the analysis of elite images of Confederation presented
in this chapter points out first the relative importance of the various
categories of environmental input in the perceptions of the elite.
Politics ranks first and economics second in both positive and negative
arguments. Geopolitics and culture exchange third and fourth positions depending on negative or positive evaluation.

In the pattern of argument on the various themes we see two
distinct styles emerge. In the one there is a direct head-to-head
confrontation of supporters and opponents. This is the case with such
themes a as political deadlock, mass public opinion, the distribution
of power between federal and provincial governments, costs, railways,
defence policy, and the preservation of French culture. On these
issues, supporters and opponents agree on the importance of the issue,
but differ over the consequences which Confederation will entail for
that issue.

The other style of argument is that which we might call selective importance, where one side or the other advances a theme either in favour of or opposed to Confederation and this line of argument is by and large unchallenged by the other side. Thus we find advanced by supporters of Confederation such themes as fear of annexation, preservation of the Imperial connection, trade and commerce, general prosperity and nationalism, while opponents stress the inability to amend, timing, and the appointment of the Upper House.

Regardless of which style of argument is employed, it is clear that no consensus was reached on the part of the political elite on the assessment of the impact of the new federal constitutional arrangement. As in discussions over any novel system, aside from projections made from past experience, respective sides tend to exaggerate the benefits and burdens that are likely to follow upon innovation. Thus, while it is clear that the elite was divided on its judgment of the new system, the factors underlying this disagreement, while reflected in the substantive arguments, may have more deep seated roots. It is precisely these socio-political correlates of support for and opposition to Confederation which we shall examine in the following chapter.

CHAPTER SIX

Socio-Political Correlates of Support and Opposition to Confederation

In the preceding chapter we sketched the main lines of argument regarding the Confederation question in order to gain an understanding of how the various attendant issues were actually perceived by the elite which had to render the decision. In this chapter we would like to carry this analysis further by attempting to identify the socio-political characteristics which distinguish supporters and opponents of Confederation overall, as well as with regard to its specific provisions. To this end, the socio-political variables discussed in Chapter 4 have been cross-tabulated with two sets of dependent variables: 1) the actual vote recorded for or against Confederation by members of the elite, giving us a summary measure of overall position; and 2) the results of the content analysis of the speeches, giving us a measure of the strength of support for or opposition to Confederation on each theme, as well as on each major category of environmental input. Analysis of these tables will allow us to identify the major support bases of Confederation *in toto*, as well as with regard to its specific features. This type of analysis allows us to examine the Confederation decision from a perspective different from traditional approaches in terms of identifying the specific nature of the groups which supported or resisted, in whole or in part, the new constitutional structure.

To begin we will discuss the relationship between vote for or against Confederation and those aspects of the elites' life profile having to do with their positions in the legislature. Here we find that among this elite support for Confederation was greater in the Assembly (63.3 per cent in favour), than it was in the Council (55.6 per cent).[1] Not surprisingly, all members of the Government voted for the measure, while the Government back-benchers and opposition among the elite split fairly evenly, 51.6 per cent in favour and 48.4 per cent opposed. In the Council, the three life members who spoke often enough to merit inclusion in the study divided two-to-one in favour of Confederation, while there was an even split among the six elected members.

The first really interesting finding concerns the relationship between the vote on the part of the members of the Assembly and the demographic characteristics of their constituencies. In addition to the over representation of mixed and urban constituencies noted in Chapter 4,[2] we find, viewing data in Table 6-1, that support for Confederation was far greater among representatives of the mixed and urban constituencies (80 per cent or more in both cases) than it was among representatives of rural ones. This distribution confirms our earlier analysis of Canadian society as one in transition, with the direction of change springing from the urban areas.[3]

TABLE 6:1 Vote on Confederation, by Type of Constituency Represented (Members of Legislative Assembly Only)

	RURAL N=19	MIXED N=6	URBAN N=5
Vote for Confederation	52.6%	83.3%	80.0%
Vote against Confederation	47.4%	16.7%	20.0%

An examination of the political party affiliation of our elite discloses a most striking variation. We see from data in Table 6-2, that opposition to Confederation was unanimous among Lower Canadian Reformers, while support was universal among Lower Canadian Conservatives. The Reform and Conservative parties of Upper Canada, on the other hand, both voted in favour of Confederation; the former registering 63.6 per cent in favour and the latter 77.8 per cent in favour.

TABLE 6:2 Vote on Confederation, by Party Affiliation (All Members of the Elite)

	LOWER CANADIAN REFORM N=9	UPPER CANADIAN REFORM N=11	LOWER CANADIAN CONSERV. N=10	UPPER CANADIAN CONSERV. N=9
Vote for Confederation	0%	63.6%	100%	77.8%
Vote against Confederation	100%	36.4%	0%	22.2%

Turning to the personal characteristics of the elite, we find first of all that ethnic background does appear related to one's vote on Confederation. Those of French ethnicity, on the whole, were slightly more prone to vote against the measure (58.3 per cent), while the members of English background were evenly divided. Support for

Confederation was primarily manifested among members of Scottish and Irish backgrounds where 75 per cent and 83.3 per cent respectively voted in favour.

An even sharper differentiation in voting patterns toward Confederation can be seen when we examine the country in which members of the elite were born. In this regard data in Table 6-3 indicate a number of interesting findings.

TABLE 6:3   Vote on Confederation, by Country of Birth (All Members of the Elite)

	LOWER CANADIAN BORN N=13	UPPER CANADIAN BORN N=8	BRITISH ISLES BORN N=14	OTHER N=3
Vote on Confederation	53.8%	12.5%	92.9%	66.7%
Vote against Confederation	46.2%	87.5%	7.1%	33.3%

Of some significance is the actual number of legislators in each category. Among Upper Canadian, Lower Canadian and British Isles natives, we see that the elite was primarily composed of those born either in Lower Canada or the British Isles. Not only were native born Upper Canadians the fewest as a major category, it is noteworthy that not one of this group included in our sample was a member of the Great Coalition.[4] In addition, the voting pattern of Upper Canadian natives on the Confederation question was most heavily negative (87.5 per cent), the only category to register an overall unfavourable verdict on the scheme. Those born in Lower Canada repeated to a great extent the pattern of division already seen previously in our discussion of ethnic origin. The fact that fully 92.9 per cent of those in the elite born in the British Isles voted in favour of Confederation clearly reveals the importance of this variable in assessing the social factors which underlay the political choice for Confederation. Thus the data on the relationship between country of birth and vote on Confederation do indeed support our earlier conjecture regarding the importance of political socialization on the founding of basic political attitudes. This importance is further supported by an examination of the connection between vote and the age of the member at the time of his landing in Canada. In this regard, of the sixteen immigrant members of the elite, the only two who voted against Confederation arrived in Canada prior to their eleventh birthdays.[5]

Religion and language are in themselves related variables and in turn they also mirror very closely the part of the province which the legislators represented. Thus while Catholics divided evenly for and against Confederation, Protestants were 73.7 per cent in favour of the scheme. On the language variable, the favourable percentage drops to 46.2 per cent among the francophone members, this difference from the religious variable reflects the presence of the English-speaking Catholic members. Anglophone support for Confederation is maintained at 68 per cent.

With regard to age, as noted in Chapter 4, the majority of our sample fell in the forty-one to fifty age group, and this dominant group voted two-to-one in favour of Confederation. There is no clear pattern of support or opposition to the measure among the younger and older age groups.

Occupation as a predictor variable of preference or aversion to Confederation is not fruitful. Among the most highly represented, the legal group, the division of opinion was almost even, (52.4 per cent in favour and 47.6 per cent opposed). Support increased among businessmen and journalists where 66.7 per cent and 60 per cent respectively voted in favour. The two farmers who appear in the elite took opposite sides, while surveyors and military officers supported the proposal unanimously.

Out of the variety of characteristics having to do with social backgrounds and political circumstances of the legislative elite selected for our study, we note that only two—party affiliation and country of birth—correlate highly with vote on Confederation.[6] In the next section we intend to investigate the relationship between these two independent variables and the major questions regarding Confederation which provided the substance of the Parliamentary debate.

A. Correlates of Support and Opposition to Confederation in the Area of Culture

Table 6:4 shows the percentage of columns in which all themes favourable and unfavourable dealing with culture appeared. These percentages are presented both by party affiliation and by country of birth. Looking first at favourable and unfavourable comments in the area of culture by party affiliation, we see striking evidence of the effect of this variable on the attitudes of the Lower Canadian members. Accordingly, we note that while Lower Canadian Conservatives expressed the most interest in culture as an argument for Confederation, their Reform counterparts found in the same subject matter the most ammunition for opposition to the proposal. Upper Canadian Reformers and their Conservative foes did not employ this category of

TABLE 6:4 Percentage of Columns in which Arguments Favourable and Unfavourable toward Confederation based on Culture Appeared, by Party Affiliation and Country of Birth

| | PARTY AFFILIATION | | | | | | | | COUNTRY OF BIRTH | | | | | |
| | Lower Canadian Reform N=10 | | Upper Canadian Reform N=11 | | Lower Canadian Cons. N=11 | | Upper Canadian Cons. N=9 | | Lower Canada N=13 | | Upper Canada N=8 | | British Isles N=15 | |
	Fav.	Unf.	Fav.	Unf.	Fav.	Unf.	Fav.	Unf.	Fav.	Unf.	Fav.	Unf.	Fav.	Unf.
No Mention	90.0	10.0	54.5	63.6	18.2	90.9	33.3	66.7	53.8	53.8	87.5	37.5	33.3	86.7
0.1% to 25%	10.0	10.0	45.5	36.4	9.1	9.1	66.7	22.2	7.7	7.7	12.5	62.5	53.3	6.7
25.1% to 50%	0	50.0	0	0	45.5	0	0	11.1	23.1	15.4	0	0	13.3	6.7
50.1% to 75%	0	10.0	0	0	9.1	0	0	0	7.7	7.7	0	0	0	0
75.1% to 100%	0	20.0	0	0	18.2	0	0	0	7.7	15.4	0	0	0	0
100% plus	0	0	0	0	0	0	0	0	0	0	0	0	0	0

TABLE 6:5 Percentage of Columns in which Arguments Favourable and Unfavourable toward Confederation based on Preservation of British Culture Appeared, by Party Affiliation and Country of Birth

| | PARTY AFFILIATION | | | | | | | | COUNTRY OF BIRTH | | | | | |
| | Lower Canadian Reform N=10 | | Upper Canadian Reform N=11 | | Lower Canadian Cons. N=11 | | Upper Canadian Cons. N=9 | | Lower Canada N=13 | | Upper Canada N=8 | | British Isles N=15 | |
	Fav.	Unf.	Fav.	Unf.	Fav.	Unf.	Fav.	Unf.	Fav.	Unf.	Fav.	Unf.	Fav.	Unf.
No Mention	100	70.0	72.7	90.9	27.3	90.9	77.8	88.9	61.5	92.3	100	100	60.0	86.7
0.1% to 10%	0	20.0	27.3	9.1	45.5	9.1	22.2	11.1	23.1	7.7	0	0	33.3	6.7
10.1% to 20%	0	0	0	0	18.2	0	0	0	15.4	0	0	0	0	0
20.1% to 30%	0	0	0	0	0	0	0	0	0	0	0	0	0	0
30.1% to 40%	0	0	0	0	9.1	0	0	0	0	0	0	0	6.7	0
40.1% plus	0	10.0	0	0	0	0	0	0	0	0	0	0	0	6.7

issues extensively, nor were there any clearly discernible trends in Upper Canadian use of this constellation of issues according to political persuasion.

The relationship between country of birth and views on the ramifications of Confederation on culture, however, yields quite different results. In this case the independent variable appears to have little effect on either positive or negative views held by the Lower Canadian representatives, while its effects among the Upper Canadians is striking indeed. Here data indicate that the native born Upper Canadians presented few arguments in the cultural area which are favourable to Confederation, and while not appearing overly concerned with the unfavourable side, 62.5 per cent did bring up negative features in the cultural area in 1 to 25 per cent of total columns. Natives of the British Isles as a whole stressed the positive side, but there were some apprehensions as well.

Within the area of culture the major specific concerns had to do with the preservation of French and British cultural values. Table 6:5 presents data on the issue of the preservation of culture serving the British interest, again by the two independent variables, party affiliation and country of birth. If we take the effects of party affiliation first, we see that it was the Lower Canadian Conservatives who offered the greatest amount of positive argument respecting the potential benefit of Confederation to preserving the British heritage. Upper Canadians of both Reform and Conservative persuasions did not comment on this issue in either direction in significant numbers. The Lower Canadian Reformers have nothing positive to offer, however, with one exception, the English-speaking O'Halloran; neither did they oppose the measure on these grounds.

An analysis of the effects of country of birth on this dimension results in few conclusive findings. It is apparent that this issue was not one which prompted the Upper Canadian natives to oppose Confederation, as they were clearly unconcerned with this particular set of consequences. As is to be expected, members who were natives of the British Isles evinced some attention to this issue, with both positive and negative implications brought into the argument. Native born Lower Canadians, in the main, attempted to allay fears that British values would be eroded by a constitutional system giving the French superiority at the provincial level.

Table 6:6, dealing with the preservation of French cultural values, reveals the intramural quarrel between the two Lower Canadian political persuasions; for we see that Upper Canadian representatives on both sides of the House, and without regard to country of birth, desist

TABLE 6:6 Percentage of Columns in which Arguments Favourable and Unfavourable toward Confederation based on Preservation of French Culture Appeared, by Party Affiliation and Country of Birth

| | PARTY AFFILIATION | | | | | | | | COUNTRY OF BIRTH | | | | | |
| | Lower Canadian Reform N=10 | | Upper Canadian Reform N=11 | | Lower Canadian Cons. N=11 | | Upper Canadian Cons. N=9 | | Lower Canada | | Upper Canada | | British Isles | |
	Fav.	Unf.	Fav.	Unf.	Fav.	Unf.	Fav.	Unf.	Fav.	Unf.	Fav.	Unf.	Fav.	Unf.
No Mention	100	30.0	72.7	0	18.2	90.9	88.9	100	53.8	53.8	100	100	60.0	93.3
0.1% to 10%	0	0	27.3	0	18.2	9.1	11.1	0	7.7	0	0	0	33.3	6.7
10.1% to 20%	0	30.0	0	0	18.2	0	0	0	7.7	23.1	0	0	6.7	0
20.1% to 30%	0	10.0	0	0	36.4	0	0	0	23.1	0	0	0	0	0
30.1% to 40%	0	0	0	0	9.1	0	0	0	7.7	0	0	0	0	0
40.1% plus	0	30.0	0	0	0	0	0	0	0	23.1	0	0	0	0

TABLE 6:7 Percentage of Columns in which Arguments Favourable and Unfavourable toward Confederation Appeared, by Party Affiliation and Country of Birth

| | PARTY AFFILIATION | | | | | | | | COUNTRY OF BIRTH | | | | | |
| | Lower Canadian Reform N=10 | | Upper Canadian Reform N=11 | | Lower Canadian Cons. N=11 | | Upper Canadian Cons. N=9 | | Lower Canada N=13 | | Upper Canada N=8 | | British Isles N=15 | |
	Fav.	Unf.	Fav.	Unf.	Fav.	Unf.	Fav.	Unf.	Fav.	Unf.	Fav.	Unf.	Fav.	Unf.
No Mention	90.0	0	36.4	45.5	9.1	90.9	22.2	44.4	46.2	46.2	87.5	12.5	13.3	66.7
0.1% to 25%	10.0	10.0	0	18.2	9.1	0	11.1	0	0	15.4	0	0	13.3	6.7
25.1% to 50%	0	10.0	0	0	9.1	0	22.2	22.2	0	7.7	0	12.5	13.3	6.7
50.1% to 75%	0	10.0	18.2	9.1	45.5	9.1	22.2	0	38.5	0	12.5	12.5	13.3	6.7
75.1% to 100%	0	10.0	27.3	9.1	9.1	0	0	0	7.7	7.7	0	12.5	20.0	0
100% plus	0	60.0	18.2	9.1	18.2	0	22.2	33.3	7.7	23.1	0	50.0	26.7	13.3

from entering the lists. Thus, for the Lower Canadians, among whom this issue was of paramount importance, we discover that the lines were sharply drawn: no Reform member views Confederation favourably on this score, and no Conservative, with the exception of the maverick, Dunkin, viewed the scheme unfavourably.

In the area of culture, which we noted in Chapter 5 was one of the environmental input categories of lesser importance, we see additional firm evidence that our two independent variables, party affiliation and country of birth, operate differently depending on whether we examine the views of Lower Canadian or Upper Canadian legislators. In the case of Lower Canada, it is party affiliation which is of singular importance, while for Upper Canada, there is some evidence that country of birth is related to views on the cultural implications of Confederation.

B. Correlates of Support and Opposition to Confederation in the Area of Politics

The political aspects of Confederation occasioned the greatest amount of debate and stirred the highest pitch of controversy between supporters and opponents of Confederation. Table 6:7 shows the percentage of total columns dealing with political concerns. Party affiliation again differentiates Lower Canadian Reformers and Conservatives, as strong support was manifested by the Conservative faction and even stronger opposition was displayed by the Reformers. Among Upper Canadian legislators, there was more favourable commentary in the area of politics than negative, and this held true for both Reformers and Conservatives, with a small group of Conservatives making very strong objections on political grounds.

With regard to country of birth, Lower Canadians again divided evenly on political questions. Among the native born Upper Canadians the tendency toward unfavourable commentary was pronounced, while favourable comment was restricted to one member. For those born in the British Isles, positive arguments out-distanced negative views by a wide margin.

The role which Confederation could play in ending the political deadlock which had developed in the legislature of the Province of Canada was the most extensively debated of all issues in the political area. As we see from data in Table 6:8, not unexpectedly, the Lower Canadian Reformers found absolutely nothing to support in the proposal, while the Conservatives of that section perceived in the scheme an acceptable solution to the revolving door politics of the Union. The

TABLE 6:8   Percentage of Columns in which Arguments Favourable and Unfavourable toward Confederation based on Political Deadlock Appeared, by Party Affiliation and Country of Birth

| | PARTY AFFILIATION | | | | | | | | COUNTRY OF BIRTH | | | | | |
| | Lower Canadian Reform | | Upper Canadian Reform | | Lower Canadian Cons. | | Upper Canadian Cons. | | Lower Canada | | Upper Canada | | British Isles | |
	Fav.	Unf.	Fav.	Unf.	Fav.	Unf.	Fav.	Unf.	Fav.	Unf.	Fav.	Unf.	Fav.	Unf.
No Mention	100	10.0	36.4	63.6	9.1	90.9	44.4	66.7	46.2	61.5	87.5	25.0	26.7	73.3
0.1% to 10%	0	10.0	0	0	45.5	0	22.2	22.2	15.4	7.7	12.5	0	20.0	13.3
10.1% to 20%	0	20.0	18.2	9.1	18.2	9.1	11.1	0	23.1	15.4	0	12.5	13.3	6.7
20.1% to 30%	0	40.0	18.2	9.1	0	0	22.2	11.1	0	7.7	0	25.0	20.0	6.7
30.1% to 40%	0	10.0	27.3	0	0	0	0	0	0	7.7	0	0	20.0	0
40.1% plus	0	10.0	0	18.2	27.3	0	0	0	15.4	0	0	37.5	0	0

TABLE 6:9   Percentage of Columns in which Arguments Favourable and Unfavourable toward Confederation based on Nationalism Appeared, by Party Affiliation and Country of Birth

| | PARTY AFFILIATION | | | | | | | | COUNTRY OF BIRTH | | | | | |
| | Lower Canadian Reform | | Upper Canadian Reform | | Lower Canadian Cons. | | Upper Canadian Cons. | | Lower Canada | | Upper Canada | | British Isles | |
	Fav.	Unf.	Fav.	Unf.	Fav.	Unf.	Fav.	Unf.	Fav.	Unf.	Fav.	Unf.	Fav.	Unf.
No Mention	90.0	70.0	36.4	81.8	36.4	90.9	22.2	88.9	53.8	92.3	87.5	62.5	20.0	86.7
0.1% to 10%	10.0	30.0	18.2	18.2	18.2	9.1	11.1	11.1	15.4	7.7	0	37.5	20.0	13.3
10.1% to 20%	0	0	27.3	0	18.2	0	66.7	0	7.7	0	12.5	0	46.7	0
20.1% to 30%	0	0	9.1	0	27.3	0	0	0	15.4	0	0	0	13.3	0
30.1% to 40%	0	0	0	0	0	0	0	0	0	0	0	0	0	0
40.1% plus	0	0	9.1	0	0	0	0	0	7.7	0	0	0	0	0

division between Upper Canadian Reformers and Conservatives on this question was much less evident. However, it was the Reformers who presented the bulk of the negative commentary.

Turning to country of birth, we find that three quarters of native born Upper Canadians in the elite found cause for criticism of the Confederation scheme on the issue of deadlock, while almost the same percentage of those born in the British Isles argued the merits of the plan as a way out of the continuing political crisis. Among native born Lower Canadians, favourable attitudes on this dimension were more widely expressed, in two cases very strongly, than were unfavourable ones.

On the question of nationalism, the most noteworthy finding when we look at the party attitudes on the question is that none of the parties spent very much energy criticizing Confederation on this score. Even the Lower Canadian Reformers, who found ample cause to attack the proposal on many fronts, made only passing and derisory comment about the potential of Confederation to create a new and great country. Moreover, Upper Canadian Reformers, as well as Conservatives from both sections, used arguments based on nationalist visions, to a much greater degree than is popularly portrayed by those who characterize Confederation as an act of political compromise devoid of high purpose.[7]

The effects of country of birth on nationalist sentiment are seen in the finding that while Lower Canadian and especially British Isles natives were frequent in their supportive comments, the Upper Canadian natives discovered in this issue fewer grounds for the strong opposition that was evident both in their vote on Confederation as well as in their attitudes on other issues.

The issue of public opinion, which revolved around whether some form of appeal to the electorate was necessary, occasioned one of the few instances of real intra party discord among the Upper Canadian Conservatives. So we see in Table 6:10 that nearly half of the Upper Canadian Conservatives in our group expressed relatively high degrees of concern over the failure to provide for popular ratification by some means, while their remaining colleagues argued less strenuously that any further form of popular ratification was not required. On this question, the Lower Canadian Conservatives did not suffer the same division within their ranks. Given the populist orientation of the Lower Canadian Reform opposition, it was reasonable to expect some vehemence in their opposition to Confederation on this question, and the distribution, where 90 per cent took their place as opponents, shows this to be the case.

TABLE 6:10 Percentage of Columns in which Arguments Favourable and Unfavourable toward Confederation based on Public Opinion Appeared, by Party Affiliation and Country of Birth

| | PARTY AFFILIATION | | | | | | | | COUNTRY OF BIRTH | | | | | |
| | Lower Canadian Reform | | Upper Canadian Reform | | Lower Canadian Cons. | | Upper Canadian Cons. | | Lower Canada | | Upper Canada | | British Isles | |
	Fav.	Unf.	Fav.	Unf.	Fav.	Unf.	Fav.	Unf.	Fav.	Unf.	Fav.	Unf.	Fav.	Unf.
No Mention	100	10.0	54.5	63.6	45.5	90.9	44.4	55.6	69.2	61.5	87.5	12.5	33.3	80.0
0.1% to 10%	0	20.0	9.1	0	27.3	9.1	11.1	0	15.4	7.7	0	12.5	20.0	6.7
10.1% to 20%	0	30.0	18.2	18.2	18.2	0	22.2	0	15.4	15.4	12.5	25.0	26.7	0
20.1% to 30%	0	20.0	9.1	18.2	9.1	0	22.2	0	0	7.7	0	25.0	13.3	0
30.1% to 40%	0	10.0	9.1	0	0	0	0	33.3	0	7.7	0	12.5	6.7	6.7
40.1% plus	0	10.0	0	0	0	0	0	11.1	0	0	0	12.5	0	6.7

TABLE 6:11 Percentage of Columns in which Arguments Favourable and Unfavourable toward Confederation based on Appointment of the Upper House Appeared, by Party Affiliation and Country of Birth

| | PARTY AFFILIATION | | | | | | | | COUNTRY OF BIRTH | | | | | |
| | Lower Canadian Reform | | Upper Canadian Reform | | Lower Canadian Cons. | | Upper Canadian Cons. | | Lower Canada | | Upper Canada | | British Isles | |
	Fav.	Unf.	Fav.	Unf.	Fav.	Unf.	Fav.	Unf.	Fav.	Unf.	Fav.	Unf.	Fav.	Unf.
No Mention	100	20.0	81.8	54.5	72.7	90.9	66.7	88.9	76.9	61.5	100	50.0	66.7	73.3
0.1% to 10%	0	50.0	9.1	0	9.1	9.1	11.1	0	7.7	23.1	0	12.5	13.3	6.7
10.1% to 20%	0	10.0	9.1	36.4	9.1	0	11.1	0	7.7	7.7	0	25.0	13.3	13.3
20.1% to 30%	0	10.0	0	9.1	0	0	0	11.1	0	7.7	0	12.5	0	6.7
30.1% to 40%	0	0	0	0	9.1	0	11.1	0	7.7	0	0	0	6.7	0
40.1% plus	0	10.0	0	0	0	0	0	0	0	0	0	0	0	0

On this issue as well as others which we have examined, country of birth differentiates clearly the Upper Canadian natives from those of the elite born in the British Isles. The native born Upper Canadians were nearly unanimously distressed with the failure to consult the people, while two thirds of those born in the British Isles argued that no such consultation was necessary. Among Lower Canadian natives, there was a tendency to stress the negative implications of the failure to consult the people.

The compromise made with the Maritime Provinces which led to the acceptance of an appointive Upper House was the subject of considerable debate by Lower Canadian Reformers who expressed concern at the sacrifice of a hard won democratic principle. Their Reform colleagues in Upper Canada likewise expressed unhappiness, although to a much lesser extent. As might be expected, the Upper and Lower Canadian Conservatives both reflected some support for the appointive principle, but the issue did not seem to generate enough excitement to cause them to have to defend it very extensively in their speeches.

Approaching the same subject according to country of birth, however, we see that it is again the Upper Canadian natives who regarded the change with the greatest degree of apprehension. A sizeable number of Lower Canadian natives had reservations as well, and those from the British Isles found least to be concerned about and most to praise. Keeping in mind, however, that British Isles natives voted in favour of the scheme with a percentage of 92.9, we see that even among this group the reversion to an appointive Upper House was not wholeheartedly accepted.

The distribution of power between the central government and the provincial governments in the new constitutional scheme, as was the case with the preservation of French culture, appears to have been a parochial issue of concern only to the Lower Canadians. For the figures in Table 6:12 show that the Upper Canadian opponents of Confederation did not find this facet of the proposals particularly objectionable. The major division was then between the Lower Canadian Conservatives, who found the distribution of powers very satisfactory, and the Reformers of Lower Canada, who viewed with alarm the potential for central government hegemony which to them seemed manifest.

Although country of birth appears less significant on this question than on a number of others, the natives of the British Isles supported the distribution of powers to a greater extent than did Upper Canadian natives. These Upper Canadians, however, did not dwell to any

TABLE 6:12 Percentage of Columns in which Arguments Favourable and Unfavourable toward Confederation based on Distribution of Power between Federal and Local Governments Appeared, by Party Affiliation and Country of Birth

| | PARTY AFFILIATION | | | | | | | | COUNTRY OF BIRTH | | | | | |
| | Lower Canadian Reform | | Upper Canadian Reform | | Lower Canadian Cons. | | Upper Canadian Cons. | | Lower Canada | | Upper Canada | | British Isles | |
	Fav.	Unf.	Fav.	Unf.	Fav.	Unf.	Fav.	Unf.	Fav.	Unf.	Fav.	Unf.	Fav.	Unf.
No Mention	100	0	63.6	90.9	18.2	90.9	66.7	77.8	53.8	53.8	87.5	62.5	40.0	86.7
0.1% to 10%	0	30.0	27.3	9.1	45.5	0	11.1	22.2	15.4	7.7	0	37.5	46.7	0
10.1% to 20%	0	30.0	0	0	27.3	0	11.1	0	23.1	15.4	0	0	6.7	0
20.1% to 30%	0	30.0	9.1	0	0	0	11.1	0	0	15.4	12.5	0	6.7	13.3
30.1% to 40%	0	10.0	0	0	9.1	9.1	0	0	7.7	7.7	0	0	0	0
40.1% plus	0	0	0	0	0	0	0	0	0	0	0	0	0	0

TABLE 6:13 Percentage of Columns in which Arguments Favourable and Unfavourable toward Confederation based on Appropriateness of Timing Appeared, by Party Affiliation and Country of Birth

| | PARTY AFFILIATION | | | | | | | | COUNTRY OF BIRTH | | | | | |
| | Lower Canadian Reform | | Upper Canadian Reform | | Lower Canadian Cons. | | Upper Canadian Cons. | | Lower Canada | | Upper Canada | | British Isles | |
	Fav.	Unf.	Fav.	Unf.	Fav.	Unf.	Fav.	Unf.	Fav.	Unf.	Fav.	Unf.	Fav.	Unf.
No Mention	100	50.0	63.6	72.7	63.6	90.9	44.4	55.6	84.6	76.9	100	37.5	40.0	73.3
0.1% to 10%	0	30.0	18.2	9.1	27.3	9.1	11.1	11.1	7.7	15.4	0	12.5	20.0	20.0
10.1% to 20%	0	10.0	18.2	0	9.1	0	33.3	22.2	7.7	0	0	25.0	33.3	0
20.1% to 30%	0	0	0	9.1	0	0	0	11.1	0	7.7	0	12.5	0	6.7
30.1% to 40%	0	10.0	0	9.1	0	0	0	0	0	0	0	12.5	0	0
40.1% plus	0	0	0	0	0	0	11.1	0	0	0	0	0	6.7	0

great degree upon the negative implications of the Federal-Provincial distribution. Moreover, some opposition by natives of the British Isles was also recorded.

Our final theme in the political area, and one which did not prompt too much debate, was that which dealt with the timeliness of instituting the new plan of Confederation. The traditional party split between the Lower Canadian Conservatives and Reformers was evident in this discussion, while the Upper Canadian Reformers tended to follow a pattern similar to that of the two Conservative factions.

When we apply the test of country of birth, however, we note that native born Upper Canadians devoted significant portions of their speeches to questioning the propriety of what appeared to be unseemly haste. Those born in the British Isles, on the other hand, expressed the greatest concern that a valuable opportunity would be lost if action were not taken expeditiously. Lower Canadian natives appear to have considered this question as not an appropriate instrument with which to promote their views whether pro or con.

An assessment of the impact of our two independent variables on the discussion of political questions discloses the difference between the factionalism of the Lower Canadian parties and the Upper Canadian parties. The cleavage between the *bleu* and the *rouge* was clearly ideological, resulting in coherent and well disciplined voting patterns, as well as a strong tendency to articulate arguments regarding Confederation according to political principle. Thus we see on virtually every political facet of the debate a division between these two Lower Canadian political persuasions.

The lesser cohesiveness of the two Upper Canadian parties owes much to the split of the Reform party when some of its members, especially George Brown, joined the Great Coalition and became co-sponsors of the proposals. Therefore it is not surprising that we find many Reformers supported Confederation in principle, while at the same time, they criticized some of its specific provisions which violate long-held Reform convictions. In the political area these were mainly the reversion to the appointive Upper House and the failure to consult the people with regard to their views on the matter.

Of more significance for Upper Canadian representatives, however, is their country of birth. For we see on most issues that those born in Upper Canada appear as a group opposed to Confederation not only in terms of their vote (87.5 per cent opposed), but also in their opposition to specific components of the Quebec Resolutions. Hence an "unconscious coalition", composed of both Reformers and Conservatives of Upper Canadian birth, seems to have emerged which

TABLE 6:14 Percentage of Columns in which Arguments Favourable and Unfavourable toward Confederation based on Economics Appeared, by Party Affiliation and Country of Birth

| | PARTY AFFILIATION | | | | | | | | COUNTRY OF BIRTH | | | | | |
| | Lower Canadian Reform N=10 | | Upper Canadian Reform N=11 | | Lower Canadian Cons. N=11 | | Upper Canadian Cons. N=9 | | Lower Canada N=13 | | Upper Canada N=8 | | British Isles N=15 | |
	Fav.	Unf.	Fav.	Unf.	Fav.	Unf.	Fav.	Unf.	Fav.	Unf.	Fav.	Unf.	Fav.	Unf.
No Mention	90.0	30.0	36.4	54.5	9.1	90.9	22.2	66.7	46.2	61.5	87.5	12.5	13.3	80.0
0.1% to 25%	10.0	20.0	18.2	18.2	27.3	9.1	55.6	11.1	23.1	15.4	12.5	12.5	33.3	20.0
25.1% to 50%	0	30.0	36.4	9.1	36.4	0	11.1	0	23.1	7.7	0	25.0	33.3	0
50.1% to 75%	0	10.0	9.1	0	18.2	0	11.1	22.2	7.7	7.7	0	25.0	13.3	0
75.1% to 100%	0	10.0	0	18.2	0	0	0	0	0	7.7	0	25.0	0	0
100% plus	0	0	0	0	9.1	0	0	0	0	0	0	0	6.7	0

TABLE 6:15 Percentage of Columns in which Arguments Favourable and Unfavourable toward Confederation based on Trade and Commerce Appeared by Party Affiliation and Country of Birth

| | PARTY AFFILIATION | | | | | | | | COUNTRY OF BIRTH | | | | | |
| | Lower Canadian Reform N=10 | | Upper Canadian Reform N=11 | | Lower Canadian Cons. N=11 | | Upper Canadian Cons. N=9 | | Lower Canada N=13 | | Upper Canada N=8 | | British Isles N=15 | |
	Fav.	Unf.	Fav.	Unf.	Fav.	Unf.	Fav.	Unf.	Fav.	Unf.	Fav.	Unf.	Fav.	Unf.
No Mention	90.0	60.0	54.5	72.7	27.3	90.9	33.3	88.9	69.2	76.9	87.5	50.0	26.7	93.3
0.1% to 10%	10.0	30.0	18.2	9.1	27.3	9.1	33.3	0	15.4	15.4	0	12.5	26.7	6.7
10.1% to 20%	0	0	18.2	18.2	27.3	0	22.2	11.1	7.7	0	12.5	37.5	26.7	0
20.1% to 30%	0	10.0	0	0	9.1	0	11.1	0	7.7	7.7	0	0	6.7	0
30.1% to 40%	0	0	0	0	9.1	0	0	0	0	0	0	0	6.7	0
40.1% plus	0	0	9.1	0	0	0	0	0	0	0	0	0	6.7	0

was decidedly hostile to the new plan. In the political area the discontent of this group was primarily registered on the issues of political deadlock and mass public opinion, and to a lesser extent on the question of timing.

At this point in our analysis the pattern of opposition and support among Lower Canadian members of the elite seems clearly based on ideology. However, the Upper Canadians present a far more complex picture, where party affiliation appears tempered by factors associated with place of birth. Support for Confederation on political grounds was concentrated among the non-natives, while the Upper Canadian natives found in the area of politics a number of issues which led them to question the scheme.

C. *Correlates of Support and Opposition to Confederation in the Area of Economics.*

In the area of economics the distribution of favourable and unfavourable commentary overall indicates that with regard to party affiliation, the intensity of Lower Canadian Reform opposition in general was less than we saw in the areas of culture and politics. The Conservatives of Lower Canada, however, spent considerable energy in advancing arguments fostering the proposition that Confederation would open the door to economic growth and prosperity. While the majority of both Upper Canadian Reformers and Conservatives found opportunity to comment on the salutary economic aspects of the new plan, in both parties a sizeable minority dissented. We see further that this minority was distinguished by the common characteristic of Upper Canadian birth. Therefore, in explaining the nature of the objections which native born Upper Canadians raised with regard to Confederation, it is apparent that economic issues loomed large. Natives of the British Isles formed the largest cluster stressing the positive economic ramifications of the new political community.

In the case of the specific economic issues trade and commerce, we see that the Conservatives of the two regions combined to present the positive brief. While those of the Reform persuasion in the two regions displayed somewhat dissimilar tendencies with regard to the affirmative argument, neither saw trade and commerce as a major weapon for attacking Confederation.

Country of birth does more to differentiate groups forwarding favourable arguments than it does unfavourable ones. In this respect, the data reveal that close to three quarters of those born in the British Isles expended various degrees of effort to maintain that trade and

TABLE 6:16 Percentage of Columns in which Arguments Favourable and Unfavourable toward Confederation based on General Prosperity Appeared, by Party Affiliation and Country of Birth

| | PARTY AFFILIATION | | | | | | | | COUNTRY OF BIRTH | | | | | |
| | Lower Canadian Reform | | Upper Canadian Reform | | Lower Canadian Cons. | | Upper Canadian Cons. | | Lower Canada | | Upper Canada | | British Isles | |
	Fav.	Unf.	Fav.	Unf.	Fav.	Unf.	Fav.	Unf.	Fav.	Unf.	Fav.	Unf.	Fav.	Unf.
No Mention	90.0	50.0	63.6	81.8	27.3	100	33.3	77.8	61.5	69.2	87.5	50.0	33.3	100
0.1% to 10%	10.0	50.0	18.2	18.2	27.3	0	55.6	11.1	15.4	30.8	12.5	37.5	46.7	0
10.1% to 20%	0	0	18.2	0	18.2	0	11.1	11.1	7.7	0	0	12.5	13.3	0
20.1% to 30%	0	0	0	0	18.2	0	0	0	7.7	0	0	0	6.7	0
30.1% to 40%	0	0	0	0	9.1	0	0	0	7.7	0	0	0	0	0
40.1% plus	0	0	0	0	0	0	0	0	0	0	0	0	0	0

TABLE 6:17 Percentage of Columns in which Arguments Favourable and Unfavourable toward Confederation based on Railways Appeared, by Party Affiliation and Country of Birth

| | PARTY AFFILIATION | | | | | | | | COUNTRY OF BIRTH | | | | | |
| | Lower Canadian Reform | | Upper Canadian Reform | | Lower Canadian Cons. | | Upper Canadian Cons. | | Lower Canada | | Upper Canada | | British Isles | |
	Fav.	Unf.	Fav.	Unf.	Fav.	Unf.	Fav.	Unf.	Fav.	Unf.	Fav.	Unf.	Fav.	Unf.
No Mention	100	50.0	54.5	72.7	45.5	90.9	44.4	77.8	69.2	76.9	100	25.0	33.3	93.3
0.1% to 10%	0	30.0	45.5	0	45.5	9.1	33.3	0	30.8	7.7	0	12.5	53.3	6.7
10.1% to 20%	0	20.0	0	9.1	9.1	0	22.2	22.2	0	15.4	0	37.5	13.3	0
20.1% to 30%	0	0	0	0	0	0	0	0	0	0	0	0	0	0
30.1% to 40%	0	0	0	9.1	0	0	0	0	0	0	0	12.5	0	0
40.1% plus	0	0	0	9.1	0	0	0	0	0	0	0	12.5	0	0

commerce would indeed be given a fillip by the proposed union. Significantly, Upper Canadian natives did not find in this particular issue cause for extended oratory of a demeaning kind. Lower Canadian natives did not appear especially concerned with either positive or negative consequences of Confederation on the trade and commerce issue, although on balance they stressed the positive features.

The issue of general prosperity invites comparison with the elites' treatment of nationalism, for here also we see an absence of trenchant criticism, as if the issue was too nebulous to grasp in any concrete way. Varying degrees of positive comment were offered by members of each party which composed the Great Coalition, with the Lower Canadian Conservatives, as they did on most issues, presenting the most sanguine expectations. Opposition on this issue was again muted, as even among the Lower Canadian Reformers, only 50 per cent had minimum negative comment to offer.

As on the question of trade and commerce, the issue was seen to be less evocative of Upper Canadian natives' adverse comment, than for instance were several of the political issues which we examined, and indeed as we shall see, on other economic issues. Natives of the British Isles again were the most lavish in their predictions of happy consequences stemming from the adoption of the resolutions.

One of the most emotional issues in the debates, and one which prompted some of the strongest language, had to do with the building of the Intercolonial Railway. The railway represented a very tangible economic commitment and was therefore treated much differently than the speculative subjects of trade and commerce and general prosperity. Party affiliation, while supplying a partial index of opposition, proved to be far less important than place of birth in explaining patterns of opposition to the construction of the railway. Support appears fairly uniform among the three government parties, although there were some dissenters within these ranks, as well as of course among the Lower Canadian Reformers.

However, an examination of views on the Intercolonial by country of birth reveals clearly the effect of Upper Canadian origin. For on this question, not one of the Upper Canadian born members of the elite ventured even a passing comment in favour of the railway, while five were quite vocal in their opposition to the building of the road. Major support for the railway was concentrated among the representatives from the British Isles and likewise this group was nearly unanimous in refraining from directing any harsh words against the railway. The issue of the railway was another which did not summon up strong feelings, either pro or con, on the part of the Lower Canadian natives.

TABLE 6:18 Percentage of Columns in which Arguments Favourable and Unfavourable toward Confederation based on Costs Appeared, by Party Affiliation and Country of Birth

| | PARTY AFFILIATION | | | | | | | | COUNTRY OF BIRTH | | | | | |
| | Lower Canadian Reform | | Upper Canadian Reform | | Lower Canadian Cons. | | Upper Canadian Cons. | | Lower Canada | | Upper Canada | | British Isles | |
	Fav.	Unf.	Fav.	Unf.	Fav.	Unf.	Fav.	Unf.	Fav.	Unf.	Fav.	Unf.	Fav.	Unf.
No Mention	100	30.0	45.5	54.5	27.3	90.9	44.4	66.7	61.5	60.0	100	12.5	20.0	80.0
0.1% to 10%	0	20.0	18.2	9.1	45.5	0	44.4	0	23.1	15.4	0	0	46.7	6.7
10.1% to 20%	0	10.0	27.3	9.1	0	9.1	0	11.1	7.7	0	0	12.5	13.3	13.3
20.1% to 30%	0	30.0	9.1	9.1	18.2	0	11.1	0	7.7	15.4	0	25.0	13.3	0
30.1% to 40%	0	0	0	9.1	0	0	0	11.1	0	0	0	25.0	0	0
40.1% plus	0	10.0	0	9.1	9.1	0	0	11.1	0	7.7	0	25.0	6.7	0

TABLE 6:19 Percentage of Columns in which Arguments Favourable and Unfavourable toward Confederation based on Geopolitics Appeared, by Party Affiliation and Country of Birth

	PARTY AFFILIATION								COUNTRY OF BIRTH					
	Lower Canadian Reform		Upper Canadian Reform		Lower Canadian Cons.		Upper Canadian Cons.		Lower Canada		Upper Canada		British Isles	
	N=10		N=11		N=11		N=9		N=13		N=8		N=15	
	Fav.	Unf.	Fav.	Unf.	Fav.	Unf.	Fav.	Unf.	Fav.	Unf.	Fav.	Unf.	Fav.	Unf.
No Mention	100	20.0	45.5	63.6	9.1	90.9	33.3	55.6	46.2	61.5	87.5	25.0	26.7	73.3
0.1% to 25%	0	70.0	0	27.3	45.5	0	11.1	22.2	30.8	30.8	0	37.5	13.3	20.0
25.1% to 50%	0	10.0	36.4	9.1	18.2	9.1	33.3	22.2	15.4	7.7	12.5	37.5	40.0	6.7
50.1% to 75%	0	0	18.2	0	27.3	0	22.2	0	7.7	0	0	0	20.0	0
75.1% to 100%	0	0	0	0	0	0	0	0	0	0	0	0	0	0
100.1% plus	0	0	0	0	0	0	0	0	0	0	0	0	0	0

Our final economic issue has to do with the costs of Confederation and their apportionment among the various provinces. On this question we see a return on the part of Lower Canadian Reformers and Conservatives to the bloc behaviour which distinguished them on most political issues. Costs and their apportionment split both of the Upper Canadian parties badly. On this issue there emerged no clear pattern, as we see no strong manifestation of either opinion for or against the financial considerations of Confederation. Of the government parties, it is only the Lower Canadian Conservatives who held together in supporting the financial arrangements of the new system.

As for country of birth, the cost of Confederation was perhaps the strongest issue which bound together those of the elite of Upper Canadian birth. Again, as was the case with railways, there was not a single positive declaration, while seven of the eight Upper Canadian natives spoke out at some length in criticism of the costs of Confederation and their allocation. In conformity with most issues, the native Lower Canadian members divided fairly evenly in positive and negative feeling, while it was the natives of the British Isles who marshalled most argument in favour of the way the question of costs had been handled.

In the economic area we find greatest support and least opposition coming from the Lower Canadian Conservatives. The two Upper Canadian parties tended to view economic issues fairly similarly, with Conservatives offering greater positive commentary. The Lower Canadian Reformers viewed the economic implications of Confederation negatively, but not strongly except on the issue of costs.

The four economic issues divide into two categories. First is the trade and commerce and general prosperity grouping where the two Conservative parties stressed the positive aspects while the opposition is not especially vocal. Second come railways and costs, where the positive case was again put by the government parties. However, on these issues we see a strenuous opposition composed of Lower Canadian Reformers and some members representing both Upper Canadian parties.

On all questions of economics the consistency of strong support coming from natives of the British Isles is noteworthy. One finds indifference on the part of Lower Canadian natives to the trade and commerce issue and the railway question as well, while on the matter of costs there was an even split pro and con. The Upper Canadian natives, while consistently opposed to Confederation on economic grounds, manifested this opposition with varying degrees of intensity. The two issues of railways and especially costs of Confederation ex-

TABLE 6:20 Percentage of Columns in which Arguments Favourable and Unfavourable toward Confederation based on Defence Policy Appeared, by Party Affiliation and Country of Birth

| | PARTY AFFILIATION | | | | | | | | COUNTRY OF BIRTH | | | | | |
| | Lower Canadian Reform | | Upper Canadian Reform | | Lower Canadian Cons. | | Upper Canadian Cons. | | Lower Canada | | Upper Canada | | British Isles | |
	Fav.	Unf.	Fav.	Unf.	Fav.	Unf.	Fav.	Unf.	Fav.	Unf.	Fav.	Unf.	Fav.	Unf.
No Mention	100	20.0	45.5	72.7	18.2	90.9	44.4	66.7	53.8	69.2	87.5	25.0	33.3	80.0
0.1% to 10%	0	20.0	9.1	9.1	27.3	9.1	22.2	0	15.4	15.4	0	12.5	26.7	6.7
10.1% to 20%	0	40.0	45.5	18.2	27.3	0	22.2	22.2	23.1	7.7	12.5	37.5	26.7	13.3
20.1% to 30%	0	20.0	0	0	9.1	0	11.1	11.1	0	7.7	0	25.0	6.7	0
30.1% to 40%	0	0	0	0	18.2	0	0	0	7.7	0	0	0	6.7	0
40.1% plus	0	0	0	0	0	0	0	0	0	0	0	0	0	0

TABLE 6:21 Percentage of Columns in which Arguments Favourable and Unfavourable toward Confederation based on Fear of Annexation Appeared, by Party Affiliation and Country of Birth

| | PARTY AFFILIATION | | | | | | | | COUNTRY OF BIRTH | | | | | |
| | Lower Canadian Reform | | Upper Canadian Reform | | Lower Canadian Cons. | | Upper Canadian Cons. | | Lower Canada | | Upper Canada | | British Isles | |
	Fav.	Unf.	Fav.	Unf.	Fav.	Unf.	Fav.	Unf.	Fav.	Unf.	Fav.	Unf.	Fav.	Unf.
No Mention	100	50.0	54.5	81.8	18.2	90.9	55.6	88.9	46.2	76.9	87.5	62.5	53.3	93.3
0.1% to 10%	0	40.0	27.3	18.2	36.4	9.1	33.3	11.1	23.1	15.4	12.5	37.5	26.7	6.7
10.1% to 20%	0	10.0	18.2	0	27.3	0	11.1	0	23.1	7.7	0	0	6.7	0
20.1% to 30%	0	0	0	0	18.2	0	0	0	7.7	0	0	0	13.3	0
30.1% to 40%	0	0	0	0	0	0	0	0	0	0	0	0	0	0
40.1% plus	0	0	0	0	0	0	0	0	0	0	0	0	0	0

cited more adverse criticism than did trade and commerce and general prosperity.

D. Correlates of Support and Opposition to Confederation in the Area of Geopolitics

Geopolitical themes ranked third in favourable comment and last in unfavourable comment among the four major categories of environmental input. Commentary on these themes followed well established patterns, as Lower Canadian Conservatives led in concentrated support, followed by the Upper Canadian Reformers and Conservatives. The Lower Canadian Reformers refrained from any endorsement of Confederation on geopolitical grounds, while 80 per cent expressed some negative feelings. While there was some slippage of support in all three government parties, the Upper Canadian Conservatives suffered the greatest amount of dissension within their ranks on geopolitical questions.

Country of birth was likewise related to views on geopolitical questions, with natives of the British Isles in the forefront of support, followed by members of Lower Canadian origin. While native born Upper Canadians generally abstained from any discussion of the positive aspects of this topic, only one having anything to say at all, a sizeable group of Upper Canadian born members uttered disapproval. However, on this set of issues, they were joined by a minority of British Isles natives and a slightly greater number of members born in Lower Canada.

On the specific issue of defence policy there was a strong showing of support from the Lower Canadian Conservatives. In contrast there was a cluster of moderate to strong criticism from their opposition among the Reformers of that section, to which was added the negative voices of three Conservatives from Upper Canada.

. Support was more widespread than opposition among those born in Lower Canada. The British Isles contingent was in the forefront of those arguing the necessity of Confederation for purposes of defence, while Upper Canadians, on the whole, had little positive to see in this line of argument. Opposition to Confederation on these grounds again seemed concentrated among those of Upper Canadian birth, although three natives of the British Isles joined in the numbers of the skeptics.

Annexation to the United States was clearly not of paramount importance in the debates. Commentary was confined to slight to moderate articulation of fears by Lower Canadian Conservatives, Upper Canadian Reformers, and Upper Canadian Conservatives. The

TABLE 6:22 Percentage of Columns in which Arguments Favourable and Unfavourable toward Confederation based on Western Development Appeared, by Party Affiliation and Country of Birth

| | PARTY AFFILIATION | | | | | | | | COUNTRY OF BIRTH | | | | | |
| | Lower Canadian Reform | | Upper Canadian Reform | | Lower Canadian Cons. | | Upper Canadian Cons. | | Lower Canada | | Upper Canada | | British Isles | |
	Fav.	Unf.	Fav.	Unf.	Fav.	Unf.	Fav.	Unf.	Fav.	Unf.	Fav.	Unf.	Fav.	Unf.
No Mention	100	90.0	72.7	81.8	81.8	81.8	66.7	88.9	84.6	92.3	87.5	75.0	73.3	86.7
0.1% to 10%	0	10.0	9.1	9.1	18.2	18.2	22.2	11.1	15.4	7.7	0	12.5	13.3	13.3
10.1% to 20%	0	0	9.1	9.1	0	0	11.1	0	0	0	12.5	12.5	6.7	0
20.1% to 30%	0	0	9.1	0	0	0	0	0	0	0	0	0	6.7	0
30.1% to 40%	0	0	0	0	0	0	0	0	0	0	0	0	0	0
40.1% plus	0	0	0	0	0	0	0	0	0	0	0	0	0	0

TABLE 6:23 Percentage of Columns in which Arguments Favourable and Unfavourable toward Confederation based on Strengthening the Imperial Connection Appeared, by Party Affiliation and Country of Birth

| | PARTY AFFILIATION | | | | | | | | COUNTRY OF BIRTH | | | | | |
| | Lower Canadian Reform | | Upper Canadian Reform | | Lower Canadian Cons. | | Upper Canadian Cons. | | Lower Canada | | Upper Canada | | British Isles | |
	Fav.	Unf.	Fav.	Unf.	Fav.	Unf.	Fav.	Unf.	Fav.	Unf.	Fav.	Unf.	Fav.	Unf.
No Mention	100	90.0	54.5	90.9	18.2	90.9	44.4	77.8	46.1	92.3	87.5	62.5	46.7	93.3
0.1% to 10%	0	10.0	18.2	9.1	45.5	0	0	22.2	23.1	7.7	0	12.5	20.0	6.7
10.1% to 20%	0	0	18.2	0	36.4	9.1	22.2	0	30.8	0	0	25.0	20.0	0
20.1% to 30%	0	0	9.1	0	0	0	11.1	0	0	0	12.5	0	6.7	0
30.1% to 40%	0	0	0	0	0	0	22.2	0	0	0	0	0	6.7	0
40.1% plus	0	0	0	0	0	0	0	0	0	0	0	0	0	0

number of Upper Canadian Reformers supporting Confederation on these grounds was counterbalanced by the number of their Lower Canadian counterparts who tended to simply reject annexation as a bogey or who argued that Confederation would hasten assimilation into the American Republic. These feelings were not, however, voiced with any great frequency.

For once the members from the British Isles did not lead the vanguard supporting Confederation, a task taken over on this issue by Lower Canadians. Characteristically, Upper Canadian natives were by and large silent with regard to the prospects of Confederation forestalling absorption into the United States, and uncharacteristically muted in their criticism of the measure on the same grounds.

The issue of development of the Northwest is interesting primarily because of its lack of salience to both partisans and adversaries of Confederation. Somewhat paradoxically, the issue generated the greatest response, both positive and negative, within the same party, the Upper Canadian Reform group. This was an issue of unique concern to Upper Canada, as we see extremely little comment by either Lower Canadian political faction.

The distribution of sentiment on Western development by those born in the British Isles and those born in Upper Canada is indeed revealing. For the data show that one of the issues which turned Upper Canadians against Confederation was the fear that commitments to solidifying the connection with the Maritimes, the Intercolonial Railway, would set back indefinitely the opening of the West. Natives of the British Isles, on the other hand, while not opposing westward expansion, saw in Confederation no impediment to its achievement.

Our final table, that dealing with the effects of Confederation on the connection between Canada and the British Empire, discloses ironically, the degree to which the Lower Canadian Conservatives gave way to positive expressions in this regard. While fewer members of the Upper Canadian Conservative and Reform Parties pointed to the benefits of Confederation in solidifying the Imperial connection, they did so with greater intensity. The Lower Canadian Reformers obviously did not concern themselves with Canada's future role in the Empire, as the smattering of opposition to Confederation as serving to weaken the imperial tie came from Conservatives of both sections.

In terms of country of birth, not surprisingly the most vehement support for this goal came from those born in the British Isles, with the concurrence of more than half of the Lower Canadian born elite. Upper Canadian opposition to Confederation cannot be interpreted as sentiment for independence, for we see that while Upper Canadians were not as exercised on this question as they were on some others, they did oppose Confederation on the grounds that it would serve to bring about independence. Thus, on this question, as on Western development, there was a clear difference in the perception of the consequences of Confederation held by natives of the British Isles as opposed to those born in Upper Canada.

To sum up our findings in the area of geopolitics, Upper Canadian Reformers maintained a favourable balance of commentary on every issue, giving most support to Confederation as bolstering defence. The Lower Canadian Conservatives, on each issue except Western development, take the lead in promoting the positive aspects of Confederation. The Upper Canadian Conservatives also supported Confederation; but manifestations of dissent were greater, particularly on questions of defence and maintaining the British connection. The Lower Canadian Reformers fail to see any merit in geopolitical arguments favouring Confederation, however, except on the issue of defence, and to some extent on the annexation question, they spent little effort attacking the scheme.

On the question of the effects of country of birth, again we see in this issue area that natives of the British Isles emerged as the leading advocates of Confederation, particularly on the sub-categories of defence and the maintenance of the British connection. The positive arguments were fewest on the subject of Western expansion. On this geopolitical issue as well, Upper Canadian natives opposed Confederation, but did so with less vehemence than they did on a number of political and economic issues. They were most negative in their opinions on the defence contribution offered by Confederation, and paradoxically feared the effects of Confederation both as hampering Western expansion and weakening the Imperial connection. Lower Canadians tended to stress the positive features of Confederation in this area and minimized its negative potential.

By way of summary, our data clearly indicate the existence of different patterns of division regarding Confederation in Lower Canada and Upper Canada. Specifically, in Lower Canada party affiliation was strongly related to both vote on Confederation, as well as articulated sentiments for and against the plan. In Upper Canada, however, the vote supporting Confederation among the elite of both parties was favourable, and while on some issues partisanship was clearly evident, a far more important characteristic in explaining support or opposition to Confederation is country of birth. While all questions discussed had national significance, some had particular salience to either region, party, or place of birth. One might have reasonably expected this to be the case with regard to the first two of these factors, but the appearance of the third, country of birth, as a predictor of interest in, and position on, particular areas of the debate, is to the best of our knowledge a factor which hitherto has gone unnoticed. Thus it is not surprising that Lower Canadians were especially concerned with issues coded under culture and also with the distribution of federal and provincial powers which directly affect the degree of provincial autonomy. In the same vein, the Upper Canadian representatives demonstrated special concern with the issues of railways, Western development, and the maintenance of the Imperial connection. The distribution of positive and negative sentiment by party affiliation certainly confirms the role of the Lower Canadian Reformers as the chief opponents of Confederation. More interesting, however, is the pattern of positive support among the three government parties, where we find Lower Canadian Conservatives the main advocates of Confederation with maximum cohesion on most questions. The two Upper Canadian parties, however, appeared much less cohesive and experienced similar problems in holding members together on the final vote and especially in the debate over key provisions. It is only when we look more closely at the pattern of desertion from the ranks of both the Upper Canadian Reformers and Conservatives, that we discover the impact of country of birth, for it is the Upper Canadian born of both parties who stand out most visibly as opponents of constitutional change, while it is those born in the British Isles who emerge as the strongest proponents. The areas in which these two groups register the greatest amount of disagreement on the question of Confederation are politics and economics. In particular the native Upper Canadians did not see Confederation solving the problems besetting the system and were concerned over the implications of the lack of opportunity afforded the population to show their feelings on the new constitution. In the economic area, the Intercolonial Railway and Western development were coupled in the minds of Upper Canadian natives as disjunctive developmental alternatives, on which the sponsors of Confederation have made the wrong choice. In addition they were very concerned with the overall high costs of the new system.

On the basis of this investigation we see that there were two major groups supporting Confederation, Lower Canadian Conservatives and both Reformers and Conservatives representing Lower and Upper Canada who had immigrated from the British Isles. With regard to opponents of Confederation, in addition to the Lower Canadian Reformers, whose position was well known, we have identified a group of Upper Canadian Reformers and Conservatives whose distinguishing characteristic is country of birth.

CHAPTER SEVEN

The Confederation Decision:
The Legacy for
the Political System

Our main purpose in pursuing this study has been to understand better the actual dynamics of the decision-making process which led to Canadian Confederation. At this point, therefore, it remains for us to summarize the major elements which contributed to the decision in the Parliament of Canada leading directly to the establishment of a federal political system. Moreover, we cannot conclude this study without attempting two tasks. The first involves an assessment of the Fathers of Confederation as political thinkers, while the second evaluates the relevance of our findings to a number of interpretations, not only of Confederation, but more generally of Canadian political developments.

In the context of the Brecher decision-making model, we identified four major components of the operational environment surrounding the Confederation decision: culture, politics, economics, and geopolitics. In the literature of Confederation all of these have been accorded importance in framing the decision. Thus, methodologically, we began by setting down the objectively determinable characteristics of the situation.

The essential feature of decision-making, however, is that actors make their judgments on the basis of their comprehension of the situation, that is, their perceptions of the environment. In short, it is necessary to have an insight into the subjective evaluation of the decision-makers. We believe that the data generated by our content analysis have provided us with the opportunity to exploit this aspect of Confederation, which has hitherto been neglected. We have rejected as unfounded any assertions that the Confederation debates are an unreliable guide to the motives underlying the decision actually taken. We find no evidence to impeach the sincerity of the speakers nor to assume any divergence between public utterance and subjective conviction.[1]

Through the content analysis of the debates we see that all aspects of the operational environment were not of equal significance in the offered for the decisions taken by a selected political elite, either to support or oppose Confederation. Specifically, political concerns dominated both positive and negative arguments, while issues in the economic area were of secondary, yet still of considerable, importance in the arguments of supporters and opponents. In favourable arguments, geopolitical issues ranked third in importance, while in negative arguments, culture outranked the geopolitical dimension. Thus in interpreting the decision, we must conclude that in the minds of those making the decision, politics and economics were the areas around which most of the debate centred.

It is to these political and economic questions that the Fathers of Confederation addressed themselves, and in doing so achieved what seemed to them solutions to their contemporary problems. These solutions, however, also provided the backdrop for the continuing problems of Canadian Federalism which have persisted to this day.

Seymour Martin Lipset, in a general commentary on democratic problem-solving, has observed the importance of solving problems as they arise in order to reduce the seriousness of cleavages and to achieve over time, effective value integration. He makes these observations in the context of three specific problems: religious differences within the polity, extension of the franchise to the working classes and the right to bargain collectively, and the question of the distribution of national income.[2] With the exception of the first, these are class oriented issues which were not prominent in the minds of the leading politicians of the Confederation period, nor were they the basis for mass movements in the Canadian political system more generally.

It is interesting to reflect on Lipset's general point about the danger of allowing problems to remain unsolved in light of the "particular and continuing problems of Canadian nationhood" outlined by Donald Smiley, and cited earlier in Chapter 2: "a) the relation between Canada and the United States, b) the relation between the English and French communities of Canada, c) the relations between the central heartland of Ontario and Quebec and those Canadian regions to the east and west of this heartland".[3] Lipset argues as if political problems, once formulated, await a definite solution, which when achieved allows for consideration of other problems. However, this conception of a political problem, as similar to a mathematical one, is not in conformity with the Canadian experience. What, for example, is the final solution to the relationship between Canada and the United States? Likewise, what solutions can be offered for the English-French conflict which would not also mark the end of Canada as a political entity or the elimination of the French-Canadian nation?

Finally, what is the solution to the economic disparities which we find across the Canadian territory? The only conclusion one can reasonably draw from these "problems" is that solutions are not to be found, but rather accommodations must be achieved. An added factor is that accommodations which are found acceptable by one generation of Canadians may be found wanting by another, and thus the recurring themes of Confederation demand the attention of successive political elites.

The importance of the accommodations achieved by the time of Confederation is that the political parameters of the problems were set and the basic political structure has endured and has manifested a flexibility which allows for the centralizing policy of a Macdonald, the recognition of provincial rights by a Laurier, and the co-operative federalism of the mid-twentieth century.[4]

Moreover, the maintenance of a political entity separate from the United States continues to be a virtually unchallenged proposition, although the means to that end are the subject of often shrill controversy. In the same vein, even spokesmen for the so-called "one Canada option" would accept some constitutionally guaranteed rights which recognize in a formal way the French-Canadian community. Thus, the continuance of a bicultural and bilingual polity is assured, unless the extreme at the other end of the spectrum, that is those separatists whose commitment to the continuance of the French-Canadian nation demands separate statehood, are successful. Even that option leaves some room for a confederal structure which might allow a viable political entity to survive.[5] Finally, the commitment made by the dominant political elite of central Canada to provide some tangible economic benefits for the peripheral segments of the country has persisted. Policies such as those embodied in the Department of Regional Economic Expansion, or oil policy which first protected the Canadian market west of the Ottawa River for the more expensive western oil, and later provided subsidies for eastern consumers for what had become more expensive imported oil, are continuing reflections of this approach.

Confederation, as the point of origin of the federal political system in Canada, must not only be seen as addressing the problems of the mid-nineteenth century, but also as creating the framework within which political issues have developed and have been debated over time. As Professor Smiley has reminded us, these major issues are for the most part variations on the original themes, and to date, the main approach has been to seek accommodation within the guidelines laid down by the Founding Fathers.[6]

A. The Fathers of Confederation as Political Thinkers

Throughout the debates the reader is struck by the very down to earth, if not pedestrian, quality of the arguments. It is a commonplace of Canadian political history to consider the founders of Confederation as lacking in general ideas about political life;[7] we are all accustomed to think of them as thorough-going pragmatists. Yet despite the dominant chorus of consequential thinking, one occasionally hears a higher note. And we shall now endeavour to write the score of these infrequently heard themes.

For the sake of simplicity we will group these themes under four headings: 1) nationalities and political integration, 2) liberalism and democracy, 3) representatives and their constituents, and 4) public policy and economic development.

NATIONALITIES AND POLITICAL INTEGRATION: John Stuart Mill, writing in 1861 on the question of nationalities and political unity, employed the term nationality, not in the narrow sense we give it today as ethnicity, but in the broad sense of homogeneity based on a united public opinion.[8] The factors which enter into the creation of such homogeneity include ethnicity and origin, linguistic community, religious community, geographical location and identity of political antecedents (which seems to mean political culture). To the extent that there is not one nationality, that is, a homogeneous society, an impediment is raised to "free institutions", for in a divided, heterogeneous society, one group is likely to dominate another. Free institutions, in this context, are obviously representative institutions or responsible government. Mill shows very little sympathy for the autonomy of the Bretons, the Welsh or the Scots. They have become part of a greater unity and the clear implication is that the greater is also the more advanced. He is unabashed in speaking of superior civilizations.[9]

His version of the principle of nationalities leads him to discuss the differences between the Flemings and Walloons in Belgium without examining their problematic co-existence in a unitary state. When he does come to speak of federal states, he indicates that they must also be based on "mutual sympathy" in regard to race, language, religion and political institutions. There is no indication given that a federal form of integration may be an appropriate institutional device for the political co-existence of groups which differ in most of the ways in which homogeneity is usually achieved. He would probably wonder what political interests they could share, other than that of defending themselves against a large, potentially aggressive neighbour.

Mill does not discuss the travails of the government under the Union. However, he speaks highly of the Durham Report, in fact takes some credit for it,[10] and undoubtedly believed in the policy of assimilation. For it is surely reasonable that inferior civilizations be absorbed in another, more superior, and he had the exuberant confidence of the nineteenth century British liberal that Great Britain was "the wealthiest, and one of the freest, as well as most civilized and powerful, nations of the earth".[11] The author of *On Liberty* apparently had little concern for the autonomous existence of inferior cultures and believed that they should bow to the fortune that allows them to be elevated to a higher stage of human development. The natives of India were also in the process of being improved in the same manner. Hence all the indications are that Mill, intensely interested in the policy of the Empire, would have seen a legislative union with a certain sphere of action relegated to local authorities as the best prescription for Canada. It would be hard to say how his solution would have differed essentially from that of John A. Macdonald.

When we see that even an enlightened liberal like John Stuart Mill saw federalism as little more than a variation of the unitary state, allowing for a degree of devolution of power, is it surprising that men whose political culture was derived in large measure from progressive British models, should not have had a higher estimation of it?[12]

In that no participant in the debates considers the possibility of the Canadian provinces becoming sovereign states, the alternatives narrow down to 1) a continuation of the existing union, 2) a legislative union either limited to the two Canadas or enlarged to include the Maritime colonies, or 3) a federal system.

A concept of equilibrium or balance of power was used by some opponents of Confederation to defend the existing political order, deadlock and all. The "little Canadians" would have been satisfied with a legislative union between the two Canadas as the answer to deadlock, but the "big Canadians", with their nationalist aspirations, wanted the Maritime colonies included in any new order. Finally, the supporters of federalism who, though in no sense convinced federalists, came to the conclusion that no other form of political integration could possibly gain the support of all the colonies involved. They bowed to necessity. Is it not ironic that Canadian federalism was not the child of political passion, but the lesser evil, reluctantly agreed to by the leaders of the Great Coalition? How reluctant this conversion

was is abundantly clear from the last minute efforts of John A.
Macdonald to change the BNA Act in London when it was being
considered by the Imperial Parliament.[13]

Thus as we shall go on to argue, Canada became a variant of what
Arend Lijphart has termed a "consociational democracy" through the
agreement of members of the two dominant ethnic elites.[14] The essence of consociational democracy consists in accommodation made
between elites without consulting the people themselves. In this case,
the mode of persuasion employed by the elites in gaining support for
a federal system of government among the electorate provides an
interesting contrast: in Upper Canada the electorate is assured that
federalism will render justice to their demand for representation according to population, while the Lower Canadian electorate is told
that their cultural heritage will in no way be diminished. Whatever
the putative merits of federalism as a form of political integration, the
Canadian instance demonstrates its attractiveness as a scheme for
having things both ways.

LIBERALISM AND DEMOCRACY: The reform agitation of the 1830s
was aimed at responsible government which implied legislative supremacy, as represented by the subordination of the executive to the
legislature. This demand was only partially realized, in the Province of
Canada, in that a portion of the Legislative Council was appointed,
thus allowing for the continuation of the anomaly that the Legislative
Council was of mixed origin. A consistent political liberalism would
have required the constitution of both Houses through election.[15]
However, the logic of liberalism had to give way before the need to
have a chamber based on federal principle, where the Maritime colonies continued to have upper houses based entirely on the principle of
appointment. The agreement on an elective upper house appears to
be the only exception made to an adherence to political liberalism.
However, as has often been remarked, to be liberal in 1865 did not
necessarily mean a commitment to democracy in the sense of the
universal suffrage.[16] As C. B. Macpherson has said, "the liberal democracies that we know were liberal first and democratic later".[17]

We turn once again to John Stuart Mill as an exemplary spokesman
of liberalism whose own thought was coming to maturity during the
years just prior to the drafting of the Quebec Resolutions. We refer to
the Mill of Considerations on Representative Government.[18] Mill undoubtedly saw the inevitability of the universal franchise in Great
Britain just as his mentor Alexis de Tocqueville had seen the inevitability of the equalization of social conditions in modern European

society. Like de Tocqueville, Mill feared the tyranny of the majority, both in society—he addressed himself to this aspect in *On Liberty*—and in the polity which is one of the leading themes of *Considerations*.

If political democracy was indeed inevitable, Mill nevertheless is a reluctant democrat. He had come to fear the prevalence of class domination in government and if he had reservations about middle class rule, he had even greater concern for the consequences of a larger and more plebian electorate. The gravamen of his argument rested on the apprehended tendency of any class to legislate on its own behalf, and in the instance at hand, for the working class to use its political power to despoil the propertied classes of their belongings. Moreover, he feared the lack of intellectual competence on the part of this new electorate to contribute to good government. In fairness to Mill, it must be said that his misgivings on the matter of competence were not limited to the working class, but extended to cover a considerable portion of the middle class as well. Nevertheless, the entrance of a large number of uneducated people into the electorate could not but exacerbate the problem.

Accordingly, Mill's prescriptions followed two lines: 1) in order to offset the tyranny of the majority, he favoured plural voting (extra votes given on the basis of education) and Hare's scheme of proportional representation. He even has some kindly words for John Calhoun and his conception of concurrent minorities.[19] 2) In order to offset the alleged incompetence of the electorate, he proposed to separate the deliberative function of parliament from the legislative function, that is, the actual drafting of legislation.

Such were the recourses to which this reluctant democrat had to appeal. Mill's significance is that he represents the transition from the old non-democratic liberalism to liberal democracy in the full sense of the term. Mill, however, had taken a step beyond Canadian liberalism. We would argue that ideologically both Macdonald and Cartier (members of the Liberal-Conservative Party) and George Brown were liberals. But they were not ready to accept the universal suffrage, perhaps mainly because of their negative perceptions of American democracy.[20] And in the light of this it is not surprising to hear leading figures in the Great Coalition characterizing democracy as mob rule, or as anarchy, or as the leveling of important social distinctions. In addition, we see them defending a purely appointive upper house in terms of having a portion of the legislative branch immune from the precipitousness and ill-conceived thought and actions of the people's representatives.

A corollary of this anti-democratic posture can be found in the government's refusal to submit the Confederation scheme to the population for their approval. Despite the argument that the people had already spoken on this matter, we are convinced that the idea of the referendum or an appeal to the people at large in the form of an election was abhorent to their elitist conceptions as it was contrary to the British tradition.

REPRESENTATIVES AND THEIR CONSTITUENTS: Although there is not a great deal to build on, the members of the Great Coalition, who do speak on the subject of representation, consider themselves to be representatives rather than delegates, or to use the current terminology of political science, they conceive of themselves as "trustees" or independent members rather than as delegates operating under instructions or a mandate in what Hanna Pitkin has called the "mandate-independence controversy".[21] While the doctrine of the mandate maintains that an unequivocal expression of the will of the majority of constituents is binding on the decision of their representatives, the doctrine of independence maintains that the member has "an obligation to look after his constituents, but not to consult or obey them".[22]

From the evidence available to us from the debates, it would be rash indeed to assume that the defenders of the trustee idea against the delegate idea would adhere to the above in its entirety. Nor would they have agreed necessarily with Edmund Burke in all the particulars which he finds implied in the conception of the political trusteeship. Yet we are convinced that the assumptions underlying the notion of the representative as independent were the assumptions of these spokesmen.

In this regard, Hanna Pitkin finds four underlying assumptions of the independence theory of representation: 1) that the representative has the responsibility of pursuing the national interest rather than any particular interest, 2) that the decision-making process is a matter of rational deliberation rather than registration of will, 3) that the representative is superior to his constituents rather than being one among equals, and 4) that the representative is a guide to the people and not just their instrument.[23] The only reservation which we have with this formulation concerns the first assumption which indicates how the trustee would conceive of his function in a unitary state, but not necessarily how he would or could conceive of it in a divided polity. Yet even with this qualification, we find that both Macdonald and Cartier speak frequently of the "national interest".[24] The rejection of the concept of the representative as a delegate is another indication of the Fathers' opposition to populist democracy. On the opposite side,

the *rouges* appealed to what they claimed were the p
tions (petitions, letters, newspaper articles, etc.) sho
opposition among the electorate to the Confederatio
ever, there is no formulation of the delegate theo
opposition spokesmen. These spokesmen did often m
however, that the subject matter of the Confederation d
just ordinary legislation. Thus it was the gravity of the ꜱᴜᴛutional
decision to be taken that necessitated an appeal to the people, not a
view of themselves as lacking the capacity to act independently on
ordinary matters, which they seemed to accept as the British Constitutional norm.

PUBLIC POLICY AND ECONOMIC DEVELOPMENT: We have discussed briefly the relationship between liberalism and democracy in
the thought of the Fathers of Confederation. We have shown, we
believe, that while the leaders of the Great Coalition were committed
to political liberalism, they objected strenuously, even harshly, to
democracy as it was perceived to function in the United States. We
can infer that the objectionable aspects of American democracy consisted in acceptance of universal manhood suffrage and also the absence of property qualifications or other criteria which would recognize social distinctions.

S. F. Wise interprets these ideas as characteristic of Conservatism or
"Toryism" and claims that the Canadian elite was only tempered in
its conservatism by the time of Confederation, rather than being, as
we have indicated, liberal.[25] We would challenge this interpretation
on two grounds.

First, the elements of liberalism that might be characterized as
conservative by twentieth century standards were commonplace in the
main stream of liberal thinkers in the nineteenth century. While many
liberals of the nineteenth century had not come to embrace what
might be considered the logical extension of liberal philosophy, e.g.,
universal suffrage, they had embraced a political ideology which was
significantly different in its essential view of man and society than was
the conservative or tory conception of social reality.[26]

In any case, and this brings us to our second point, our findings
have indicated that the ideas which most significantly influenced the
Confederation decision found their genesis, not in the native soil of
Canada, but rather came from mid-Victorian England. It was the
views of immigrants from that milieu rather than those of native sons,
which carried the most weight in framing the compromise which
Confederation represented.

to economic liberalism, in 1865 it came to be identified with the doctrine of the Manchester School which had gained increasing influence since its inception at the time of the Anti-Corn Law League. The conventional view of the Manchester School of economic liberalism is that it was based on classical economics, *laissez faire*, and particularly, the idea of free trade.

On the basis of their consistent criticism of the Manchester School one might infer that the leaders of the Great Coalition rejected economic liberalism in its entirety. This would hardly be a surprising view on the part of colonials toward a theory held in the metropole to the effect that the costs of maintaining colonies outran the benefits. However, there is a common misunderstanding that mid-nineteenth century British liberals of the kind who would have supported free trade, were also opposed to government financing and control of internal improvements, and that accordingly a coalition government which supported a policy of national expansion under government and financing from the public treasury could not have been liberal in the economic sense. Hence it is important to refer to the statements of leading British liberals on this issue. The view that public expenditure for internal improvements was not incompatible with liberalism was stated by Thomas B. Macaulay in a speech to the House of Commons in 1846. Macaulay said that it was a misunderstanding of the principle of non-interference which prevented those who should act on behalf of the nation from supporting public transportation. "Consequently, numerous questions which were really public [and he is referring specifically to the railway] questions which concerned the public convenience, the public property, the public security, were treated as private questions. That the whole society was interested in having a good system of internal communications seemed to be forgotten."[27]

Again, from a more familiar voice, that of Goldwin Smith, the great defender of the Manchester School, we are told that "What services government should undertake, whether it should own the railways as well as the highroads, and telegraph as well as the post, whether it should build in private yards or in yards of its own, is not a question of principle ... ".[28] Let it be added of course that Smith showed a clear preference for relying on voluntary associations for social initiatives though he would surely agree that where the expense involved was beyond the resources of private persons, progress should not be impeded.

Surely such staunch spokesmen for nineteenth century liberalism were expressing common liberal convictions rather than merely eccentric views. Our point is that the public policy advocated by the members of the Great Coalition, with its extensive program of public works, is not necessarily a departure from liberal economic thought at the time. The way in which public financing and public enterprise were combined in the actual execution of transportation policy adds support to this assertion. The difference between supporters and opponents of Confederation did not turn on whether the government should take initiatives in this sphere, but rather concerned which plans were more urgent for future economic growth. The government saw the immediate need for a rail link with the Maritime provinces, while the Upper Canadian opponents of Confederation thought that westward expansion should have priority. Clearly then, this was not a conflict over economic ideology, but rather a conflict of interests.

B. Interpretations of Canadian Political Development

If the foregoing represents the way in which the Fathers of Confederation perceived some of the major political issues of the day, how in turn, has their decision to form a federal political system been interpreted by later writers on Canadian political development? In the following section, five interpretations will be examined: 1) the fragment theory of Louis Hartz, 2) the counterrevolutionary origins theory of Seymour Martin Lipset, 3) consociational interpretations, 4) economic interpretations, and 5) geopolitical interpretations.

THE FRAGMENT CULTURE INTERPRETATION OF LOUIS HARTZ:

With regard to the cultural interpretation of Canadian political development the most pertinent theory and the most influential has been the Hartz theory of fragment development. Originally conceived in the context of American political development,[29] the theory was subsequently expanded to encompass the development of a number of political systems which shared the common attribute of having been founded by European immigration.[30]

Summarized briefly, Hartz envisions change in the European mother countries occurring through a dialectical interaction, wherein feudal and liberal ideologies compete for dominance and in turn give rise to a socialist ideology, so that no one ideological tendency is capable of exercising hegemony.[31] In such a perspective, each ideology is conditioned by the others in the culture. In contrast to this situation of ideological competition in the parent cultures, Hartz maintains that the fragment culture, precisely because of the selective character of immigration and its relative isolation, unfolds its potentialities or its teleology only within the confines of its founding value structure.[32] He can then argue that the fragment cultures present us with instances of "pure" ideological evolution, as opposed to the contagion or interaction model characteristic of Europe, wherein ideologies give birth to one another over time.

The specific application of the Hartz theory to Canada has been made by Kenneth D. McRae, where he developed the Hartzian thesis that within Canada there are in fact two founding fragment types giving rise to distinct value structures, the feudal in French-speaking Canada and the liberal in English-speaking Canada.[33] McRae was in agreement with Hartz' explanation of the dynamics of change, or more appropriately non-change, and argued further that English Canada is essentially liberal as Hartz argued America was liberal. McRae asserted that there were but minor ideological differences between the American revolutionaries of 1776 and the United Empire Loyalists who immigrated to Canada because of the revolution.[34] It is on the question of the ideological composition of the English-Canadian fragment that Gad Horowitz takes issue with Hartz, or more specifically, with McRae. Horowitz argues that either sufficient "tory" or "feudal" ideas were brought into Canada by the United Empire Loyalists,[35] or that the basic ideological "set" of the English-Canadian value structure had not congealed until after 1815, by which time socialism had been incorporated into the "fragment nationalism" of English Canada through immigration from the British Isles.[36] Whatever the cause, for Horowitz, socialism is a legitimate and viable political movement in Canada, while in the United States it is not.

The Hartz thesis, positing a single variable explanation of development, as elaborated by McRae and Horowitz, can be attacked on two grounds. The assumption that there are two kinds of political development, one of which is dialectical and the other evolutionary, can be questioned first by examining the history of European political development itself. If isolated political cultures are said to evolve in a pure way, that is in such a way that their potentialities are manifested over time, how does it happen that European feudalism developed the competitive political culture characteristic of modern European states?

The second ground for criticizing the Hartz thesis, the one which we have stressed, is the empirical application of the theory to Canadian political development. Specifically, we have in the original exposition of the Hartz theory and in the debate between McRae and Horowitz over its application in Canada, two propositions which are empirically testable in the context of an examination of Canadian Confederation. The first pertains to the duality of political culture in Canada. Since English Canada and French Canada serve as examples of Hartz' "liberal" and "feudal" fragment types, it would appear to us that an empirical test of the validity of Hartz' theory can be found in the Confederation of the British North American Provinces, where the two fragment types debated the constitutional arrangement that would establish the ground rules for their mutual co-existence. It is our contention that if there is power in Hartz' argument regarding the persistence of founding political cultures over time, we should, in examining debates on Canadian Confederation, find a significant variation between attitudes toward Confederation on the part of native born French-speaking Lower Canadians, a "feudal" fragment, on the one hand, and native born English-speaking Upper Canadians, a "liberal" fragment on the other. We should as well expect a cohesiveness of views within the two fragment types. Second, with regard to the dispute between McRae and Horowitz, we can examine those views toward Confederation held by native born Upper Canadians as opposed to those held by immigrants from the British Isles in order to ascertain the degree of difference between the two groups and to determine which was most influential in molding the new political system which emerged in Canada in 1867.

Data on socio-political correlates analysed in Chapter 6, point out that there are indeed sectional differences in the degree of support for Confederation, with Upper Canada providing the bulk of the favourable votes. However, among our elite sample, we fail to detect the degree of cohesiveness of opinion within either of these two sections, which one should have expected if the Hartz theory held true. What the data do clearly show is that within both fragments, there were important cleavages. Furthermore, within the feudal fragment these differences appear to be based on ideology rather than to be variations within a group which displays a common fund of values.[37] In the Upper Canadian fragment the division is between native and foreign born, and in this case our data indicate that the members born in the British Isles led the argument in favour of Confederation, while Upper Canadian sons were the most vocal against the constitutional change.

Clearly, then, our study makes a number of strong points regarding the Hartz theory and its application to Canada. First, the divided character of the "feudal fragment" is not what one would expect given the Hartz thesis. Indeed, we found some of the strongest declarations in defence of liberal ideas to have emanated from the *rouge* spokesmen of Lower Canada. At the same time, from the same fragment, there are manifestations of very conservative attitudes, particularly in regard to democracy, which need not necessarily be categorized as feudal. Nevertheless, the predominant pattern is one of division so deep as to constitute an ideological conflict totally out of keeping with the coherence which should characterize the elite of a fragment culture such as that of mid-nineteenth century French Canada, which Hartz cites as an exemplary case of the purity of fragment cultures.[38]

Second, in the area of Upper Canada, the degree of cohesiveness among native born "liberals" does provide some validation of Hartz' assumption regarding the persistence of founding fragment traits. However, within this same group, we see much stronger evidence of the failure of the founding culture to assimilate immigrant groups and subsume their beliefs within the official ethic of the indigenous group. Thus, on this question, our data furnish evidence that tends to confirm the propositions put forward by Horowitz that an early congealment of Upper Canadian values had not occurred. Our findings are also consistent with an alternative explanation, the "transit of civilization" theory, in that considerable influence continued to be exerted by elements outside the context of the fragment population.[39] Indeed, the intellectual influence of mid-nineteenth century Britain continued to have a most significant impact on the ideas which were current among the elite and which determined the nature of Confederation. This is hardly surprising in a colonial setting.

THE COUNTERREVOLUTIONARY INTERPRETATION OF SEYMOUR MARTIN LIPSET: Whereas Hartz explains English-Canadian development in terms of its fragment origins as an offshoot of a homogeneous American liberalism, Seymour Martin Lipset sees the effect of the American Revolution in a different light. He counterposes the United States and Canada as examples of revolution and counterrevolution respectively, and the development of Canadian political culture is seen as a reaction to the American Revolution.[40]

Lipset arrives at this conclusion by first adopting the Parsonian pattern variables as the basis for his comparisons of Canadian and American value structures. Four specific dimensions are investigated: ascription-achievement, particularism-universalism, collectivity orientation-self orientation, and elitism-equalitarianism. On these dimensions Lipset sees Canada as more ascriptive, particularistic, collectivity oriented and elitist than the United States.[41]

In explaining the causes of these differences, Lipset isolates three variables: 1) the "counterrevolutionary beginnings of Canada", 2) differences in religious organization in the two countries, and 3) differences in the character of frontier life brought about by the prior presence of government in the Canadian case.[42] While our study has no relevance to the latter two causes, we feel that with regard to the counterrevolutionary origins of Canada, our study does provide data which allow us to probe the validity of this assertion.

More generally, however, before examining our data in light of the Lipset explanation, we would argue that Lipset in his analysis of the United Empire Loyalists has mistakenly equated being against the separation of the American colonies from Great Britain with being "counterrevolutionary" in the sense that Edmund Burke is ordinarily seen as the prototype of the modern counterrevolutionary. Indeed, one developmental explanation would argue that there was no real revolution to be counterrevolutionary against, in that a major social upheaval did not take place, rather there occurred a war of national liberation. Accordingly, the Loyalists were not significantly different in their dominant political culture than those who supported the revolution.[43]

The debates on Canadian Confederation which occurred some ninety years after the American Revolution, to our minds offer no evidence which would substantiate the Lipset thesis of what dominant political cultural strains were supposed to have been established with the coming of the United Empire Loyalists to Canada. For one thing, the French Canadians, whom Lipset leaves out of his consideration, reflect a set of values which is not derived from a previous American experience. The *bleu* members among the French ranks were the most tradition-minded. They clearly distrusted democracy and feared the consequences of American hegemony to French cultural survival. In this sense they came the closest to being "counterrevolutionary", and if there was any group that would have been favourable to turning back the modern tendency toward democracy, it would have been these gentlemen.[44]

Their *rouge* counterparts, however, appeared to be the strongest exponents of democracy who entered into the debate. Their attitudes may well have been influenced by the American experience, but not in the way that Lipset suggests, for their American models would have been found in the Jacksonian movement, which was the heir to the more radical tradition in the United States.

It is not fanciful to compare the *bleu-rouge* controversy in Lower Canada with the Whig-Jacksonian debate in the United States, excepting of course the issue of monarchy. It is important to note, however, that while the Jacksonians had achieved a wide measure of success in the 1830s, the *rouges* of the 1860s were unable to gain acceptance of their ideas in the Confederation agreement. In fact, the party had already passed its political apogee prior to Confederation.[45]

While in the case of Lower Canada the conservative, if not counter-revolutionary, position prevailed in the Confederation decision, with regard to Upper Canada the situation is far more complex. As we have noted, in Upper Canada the major support for Confederation came from those born in the British Isles. Examining the reasons advanced for supporting constitutional change, in the main we see this group focusing on three issues: 1) Confederation as a formula for extricating the country from prolonged political deadlock, 2) as a step toward promoting national unity and greatness within the context of the Empire, and 3) as fostering trade and economic prosperity. These arguments not only fail to be counterrevolutionary, but in fact are forward looking in the line of nineteenth century expansionist British liberalism.[46]

While the minority opinion in Lower Canada was reformist, with emphasis on the political aspects of the debate, the minority opposition in Upper Canada, while sharing these reformist political views, concentrated more on the economic side of the question. They found themselves in the paradoxical position, as a liberal group, of defending the status quo against changes which they believed would benefit other parts of the country to the detriment of Upper Canadian parochial interests. On the political side they were cautious democrats, in that they supported an appeal to the people, were opposed to an appointive Upper House, and criticized the haste with which the Confederation project had been undertaken.

Much more important, however, for the native born Upper Canadian opponents, was a distrust of the economic implications of the new arrangement. They were particularly adverse to the railway policy which they saw as open to corruption and misplaced in terms of developmental priorities—it favoured the east rather than the west—and with the amount as well as the distribution of debt within the new federation. Here we have the first instance within the context of Confederation of a group of central Canadian legislators recoiling from the prospect of having their constituents subsidize development in distant and less favoured regions. Following from this analysis, it is wrong to characterize this opposition group as counterrevolutionary. Rather, we would describe them as essentially parochial nineteenth century liberals, distrustful of sweeping changes in the status quo.

Of the four distinct groups which emerged from our analysis of the Confederation debates, only one has the characteristics which Lipset assigns to the Canadian political culture as a whole. This group, the French-Canadian conservatives, however, has no ideological link with the American Revolution and Loyalist immigration to Canada. Their conservatism is a reflection of a traditionalist value structure which emphasizes ascription, particularism, collectivism, and elitism. Moreover, we take issue with Lipset's identification of groups possessing these attributes as counterrevolutionary. On the whole the British North America Act cannot be characterized as a sliding back from the general thrust of democratic development in the English-speaking world in the mid-nineteenth century. The one example of "regression" is the adoption of an appointive Senate rather than an elected one. But this can be seen more as a testimony to the need to compromise with the existing practice in the Maritimes rather than based on theoretical justification as a check on the popular will.[47] More generally, while the BNA Act did not address itself to democratic principles which were current in contemporary American experience, such as extension of the franchise and the number of elective offices, this does not by any means indicate that it is counterrevolutionary in orientation.[48]

One might argue, indeed, that the need to accommodate a bicultural environment precludes the development of a homogeneous society. In this regard, the lesser liberalism of English Canada is not necessarily due to the persistence of Tory ideas, but rather to the necessity of compromising with the more conservative values of French Canada. For instance, the divorce rate, one of the indicators which Lipset uses to characterize Canada as more traditional and conservative, may owe less to the cultural values of English-speaking Canadians than to the fact that French Canada has influenced the legal basis for divorce in the country.

THE CONSOCIATIONAL INTERPRETATION: A third theory of political development which deals with the interrelationships between culture and politics is that of consociational democracy as developed by Arend Lijphart. In attempting to explain why some polities which are culturally fragmented are at the same time politically stable, Lijphart focuses on the need for accommodative behaviour on the part of competing elites. According to Lijphart,

> The leaders of rival subcultures may engage in competitive behaviour and thus further aggravate instability, but they may also make *deliberate efforts to counteract the immobilizing and unstabilizing effects of cultural fragmentation.*[49]

While rival elites must see the wisdom of making compromises and have the power to "sell" these compromises to their followers, at the mass level, Lijphart argues that for the consociational model to work, there should be clear boundaries between the subcultures as "conflict arises only when they are in contact with each other."[50]

Before Lijphart formally applied his theory to Canada, applications were made by S. J. R. Noel, Robert Presthus, and Kenneth D. McRae. Noel, in commenting on a paper given by Lijphart at Laval University and later reprinted in the *Canadian Journal of Political Science*,[51] offers the opinion that the theory suggests

> the lack of a pan-Canadian identity combined with strong regional subcultures is not necessarily a dysfunctional feature in terms of the successful operation of a federal political system, as long as within each subculture demands are effectively articulated through its political elite. Secondly, it suggests that in the relative absence of a national mass consensus Canadian federalism has been maintained and made to work mainly through a process of accommodation at the elite level.[52]

Robert Presthus, arguing from contemporary data, emphasizes the role of elites in the private sector, in conjunction with those in the political structure, in constructing accommodative policies.[53] Presthus sees the system as essentially consociational, and cites as evidence accommodative practices regarding Cabinet appointments, federal-provincial relations, civil service appointments, the Supreme Court and the Senate.[54] According to Presthus:

> Certainly, recent history indicates the critical role of accommodation politics at the highest level: the felicity with which the Liberals under Pearson played this part of the game, contrasted with the ineptitude of the Conservatives under Diefenbaker underscores the electoral consequences of neglecting Quebec.[55]

While Kenneth McRae's overall assessment is that "the existing Canadian political system, even at best, must be viewed as a very imperfect example of consociational democracy",[56] his survey of the period from the establishment of the Union and responsible government to Confederation is framed in terms of the Lijphart theory. The government of the Union, which was remembered as a period of instability and deadlock, marked a time when the politics of elite accommodation was particularly central to the government, but failed because of the absence of clearly delineated boundaries between the two groups.[57] According to McRae's analysis, the Great Coalition, composed of Lower Canadian Conservatives and Upper Canadian

Conservatives and Reformers, was formed for "the explicit purpose of breaking the deadlock through radical constitutional reform".[58] The deadlock was broken by the granting of provincial autonomy to the two founding groups in an attempt to minimize conflict on issues of cultural concern at the "national" level.

Lijphart's own classification of Canada as a "semi-consociational democracy"[59] is based heavily on the work of McRae, Presthus, and Noel. While asserting that conditions in Canada are not conducive to consociational practices,[60] he nevertheless reviews the extent to which Canada has manifested consociational behaviour in the four categories of structures which are recognized as consociational: segmented autonomy, the "double majority" principle, rules of proportionality, and grand coalition.[61]

While there is disagreement that contemporary Canadian political practice resembles consociationalism closely enough to be discussed usefully in terms of the model, or that it would be normatively beneficial if Canada were to become more consociational,[62] our data certainly confirm the description of Canada as at least a variant of consociational democracy at the time of Confederation, and allow us to explore further the historical interpretations offered by McRae. First, it must be noted that elite accommodation at Confederation took place at two distinct levels: 1) between Canada and the Maritimes, and 2) between the two sections of Canada.

With regard to the former, the rather unexpected arrival of the delegation from the United Canadas at the meeting of Maritime politicians and the subsequent agreement on a formula for political integration of the Colonies is a striking example of political accommodation, though more on the lines of international agreements than the internal accommodation usually referred to by the consociational theorists. In this instance, where the cultural diversities were much less important than economic and political questions, the arrangement made by the elites was not accepted without considerable opposition from the natives of the Maritime provinces. And the temporary repudiation of the signers of the pact by the voters of New Brunswick was seized upon by opponents of Confederation in Canada as indicating the absence of popular support for the measure. Hence the contrast between an arrangement made between political elites working without instructions and popular reaction is significant, for it can be argued that the politics of elite accommodation is a method by which decisions are made, which as far as possible must avoid popular consultation and agitation, which are perceived as destabilizing.

With regard to this last point, the Government of Canada would not allow any changes to be made in the Quebec Resolutions either by amendment or by submitting the measures to the electorate. The justification for this was the time honoured one that treaties must be accepted or rejected in their entirety.[63]

It is important to note, however, in the working of elite accommodation that the accommodationists were opposed by a minority who objected to various aspects of the compromise. In the Canadian-Maritime compromise this involved questions of representation, various financial provisions, the Intercolonial Railway, and the appointive principle with regard to the selection of the Upper House. On each of these questions, members of our political elite attacked the terms of agreement, and significantly members of the government responded by alluding to areas where the Maritimers felt the compromise did not favour them.[64]

The English-speaking non-accommodationists found fault with the particulars of the scheme because they favoured a majoritarian principle, and if they were to be allied with the Maritimes in any way or continued to be joined with Lower Canada, they wanted a majoritarian principle, that is, "rep. by pop". French-Canadian non-accommodationists, on the other hand, feared any agreement which might jeopardize their position and were content, therefore, to live with the status quo in which their interests were guaranteed.

If the accommodation reached at Charlottetown was one basically between regions, the debate in the Parliament of Canada dwelt more upon relations between the founding ethnic groups. Here the politics of elite accommodation is most visible, and is symbolized by two names: George Brown and George Cartier. Brown, the leader of the Upper Canadian Reform movement, notorious critic of French-Canadian ways, and chief promoter of "rep. by pop.", steps forth as a peacemaker, expounding the virtues of compromise.[65] Cartier from the French side, whose background was with the centrifugal tendencies of French-Canadian society,[66] likewise emerges as the apostle of accommodation leading to increased harmony between the founding peoples. Particularly noteworthy in this regard are his frequent tributes to the loyal and honourable qualities of the French-Canadian population, with specific assurances that the Protestant minority in Lower Canada would be dealt with fairly.[67]

In contrast to the issue orientation of opposition with regard to the accommodation with the Maritimes, the non-accommodationists in the English-French controversy unleash virulent *ad hominem* attacks on the two men for their supposed abandonment of principle. It is hard to tell which gentleman comes under the most scathing attack.

Cartier is castigated as a pygmy and a traitor,[68] while Brown is accused of having sold out for high office.[69]

As our analysis in Chapter 6 indicated, elite accommodation in the English-French area was made easier because the question was not perceived as particularly salient by the English-Canadian members. The dispute was really between the two factions within Lower Canada. Thus the existence of two main lines of opposition to accommodation, the political-economic with regard to the Maritimes and the cultural with regard to the two sections of Canada, tended to split the non-accommodationists into two camps. This split is especially evident with regard to the issue of "rep. by pop.", where Upper Canadian non-accommodationists favoured it and attacked George Brown for failing to press for the principle, while the Lower Canadian non-accommodationists saw in the scheme a disguised legislative union in which their culture would be submerged.

Thus in the debates on Confederation it is possible to see the emergence of a distinctive style of Canadian decision-making which is based on the practice of elite accommodation[70] as opposed to populist methods of consultation such as the referendum. Moreover, this style has persisted as there is a rather strong parallel between the claims made by the participants in the Quebec Conference that the resolutions agreed upon were in the nature of a treaty and could not be altered by legislators, and the present situation where leaders of the Federal and Provincial governments gather at Conferences of First Ministers and whatever agreements they achieve are presented as *faits accomplis* to their respective legislatures.[71]

ECONOMIC INTERPRETATIONS OF CONFEDERATION: While Charles Beard's thesis, contained in his *An Economic Interpretation of the Constitution of the United States*,[72] was widely criticized as an attack on the high mindedness of the American Founding Fathers, even by those who shared his general value orientation, Canadians have never been particularly shocked by the imputation of economic motives to the participants in the Confederation debates.[73] Although it is true that the nefarious machinations of the Grand Trunk were frequently evoked in partisan rhetoric, the idea that economic interest and economic development had a determining influence on the Confederation decision has been also advanced by serious scholars of the period.

W. A. Mackintosh, in an early article, analyses the results of Canadian western expansion to the waters of Lake Huron and Georgian Bay on the Confederation decision. On the one hand, he argues that this expansion necessitated the political readjustment which Confederation represented.[74] On the other hand, he points out that the influence of the western frontier (then represented by the newer sections of Upper Canada) was not comparable to that which had emerged in the contemporary United States. Whereas the political interests of the American West were represented by the victorious Jacksonian movement, in Canada the combination of Montreal based commercial interests, economic and geographical impediments, combined to frustrate a western dominance in the new federation.[75]

A more broadly based interpretation is offered by Donald Creighton. Creighton's view is that the rise of industrialization provided the impetus for territorial expansion, political union, and centralization in many countries in the mid-nineteenth century, Canada included. Successive decisions, therefore, beginning with political union, but leading to westward expansion, transcontinental railways, and the imposition of a protective tariff, were not mere coincidence.[76] In Creighton's analysis, Confederation was dedicated to the construction of a national economy which would recreate the advantages which had been provided first by preferential trade with Great Britain and subsequently by reciprocity with the United States.[77]

A more recent neo-Marxist analysis is provided by R. T. Naylor. He emphasizes that the Canadian economy of the day was dominated by merchant and finance capital rather than industrial capital, and thus the Fathers of Confederation were trying to perpetuate a mercantilist system in which Canada would remain basically colonial in its economic organization. He cites the advantages to be gained by British bond holders of both government and railway debentures as the real impetus for Confederation. Indeed, he identifies the Baring Brothers as the true Fathers of Confederation.[78] This public finance view of Confederation is further developed by Naylor in his more recent work, *The History of Canadian Business*.[79] While this interpretation of Confederation may be extreme, it is none the less true that the economic involvements of the Fathers of Confederation were for the most part not in the industrial sector, which both Naylor and Creighton point out was incipient at best.[80]

While Naylor feels that merchant-finance capitalism has remained the basis of the Canadian economic system, Creighton argues that the "national policy" embodied in a high protective tariff and inaugurated in the decade following Confederation, constituted the culmination of the Canadian development towards an industrial state on the model of the United States.[81]

When we look at these economic interpretations of Confederation in light of our study, the first point to be made is that economic issues were indeed important in the views of those who were actually making the decision. Second, there is a distinct dichotomy between those emphasizing the economic advantages to accrue from Confederation and those denigrating the economic forecasts provided by the government. In this regard, our findings indicate that those taking part in the debate and using economic arguments were only partially concerned with these macro-economic considerations. Indeed, the most hostile groups, the Lower Canadian reformers and the native born Upper Canadians, both seemed most concerned with the effects of the Confederation scheme on public finances. Frequently their only mention of the overall trade and commerce aspects of the arguments were in the form of ridicule rather than any closely argued economic theory. However, where they did deal in very precise figures was with regard to the distribution of debt and other costs associated with the bringing of the Maritimes into the new union. Part of this cost, it is true, would be incurred by the building of the Intercolonial Railway, which was, in part at least, a facet of the grand economic scheme of the proponents of Confederation. But even in that regard, criticism was couched in terms of the long held hostility towards the Grand Trunk and its principles rather than being a response to a more generalized economic argument.

On the other hand, the chief spokesmen for Confederation did concentrate on the overall promise of prosperity based on increased trade and commerce that would result from the establishment of a new economic system. These arguments stressed the development of markets to be created by the union, the advantages to be gained by a land route to the Atlantic, and the ease with which foreign capital could be obtained. These arguments were couched in terms of contemporary economic statistics rather than in the language of economic theory.

From the foregoing, it is clear that the debates themselves were not argued in terms that lend themselves to verification of the motives attributed to the Fathers by Naylor,[82] although the more general comments of Creighton regarding the need to create an alternative economic order are corroborated. Naylor's assertion that the Confederation decision hinged on the question of public finance cannot be substantiated by reference to the Confederation debates themselves. For while issues of public finance were mentioned, and in some detail, they cannot be said to have taken pride of place in the arguments adduced pro or con regarding Confederation. As for Mackintosh's arguments, we do indeed see evidence in the debates of the recognition of the need to deal with the concerns of Upper Canada, particularly western expansion. At the same time, however, it is obvious that the prescriptions offered by the native born Upper Canadians for economic and political settlements remained minority ones. This is most clearly seen in the debate over whether the building of the Intercolonial Railway would draw scarce resources and interest away from the northwest territories.

It is evident from our findings that economic considerations were near the forefront of the concerns of the Fathers of Confederation. But what is less evident in the economic interpretations of Confederation is the degree to which this interest centred on public finance rather than economic development. While it may be that the proponents of Confederation argued for the creation of a new economic system, its detractors responded with arguments which focused essentially on the more mundane question of how much it was going to cost and who was going to foot the bill.

GEOPOLITICAL INTERPRETATIONS OF CONFEDERATION: The last general complex of explanations which we would like to deal with is that which emphasizes the effects of political geography and international relations. There are two interrelated components to this set of explanations; one dealing with the imperial connection between Canada and Great Britain and the second dealing with cross border relations with the United States. These two intersect primarily because of the hostility in the United States towards British policy during the American Civil War.

With regard to the Imperial connection, the pressures on Great Britain, in Europe as well as in North America, led not only to strengthening of the free trade assumption that the cost of maintaining colonies outweighed benefits of possession, but also precluded the diversion of men and material to defend the colonies from more urgent requirements in Europe. Thus the military requirements reinforced policy which Great Britain had entered upon some years earlier. In the interpretation of C. P. Stacey, Confederation, for Great Britain, was seen as a means whereby responsibility for defence could be placed more squarely on the shoulders of the united colony and British forces made available for operations in the European theatre.[83]

Defence, of course, meant defence against the United States. In the event of any hostilities between the United States and Great Britain, Canada was sure to become a battleground. Not only was aggression from the United States feared as a consequence of anti-British feeling, but also Canadians feared their neighbour's propensities for territorial expansion under the label of "manifest destiny".[84] A number of these trends are drawn together by Robin Winks as follows:

> The war helped illustrate to the Colonial Office that some other form of government for the series of disconnected North American colonies was essential, and it revealed the hostility that existed between those colonies and the Northern states.... But the Civil War was beneficial to Canada, for it promoted British North American unity in at least four ways. The possibility of an American invasion made union a means to a more effective defense. With the loss of reciprocal trade with the United States the colonies needed to band together to develop complementary markets. The war furnished a respite from American expansionism, which gave the counter-expansionism of Canada West an opportunity to move towards eventual absorption of the Red River district. And the spectacle of war provided a potent object lesson in statecraft and constitution-making that Canadian leaders did not ignore.[85]

The content analysis of the debates which we have carried out reveals that these considerations have definitely less significance than domestic political and economic concerns, in that geopolitics ranked last in terms of opposition arguments and behind politics and economics in positive arguments.

The spokesmen for the government consistently maintained that Confederation would preserve the Imperial connection, while some members of the opposition saw it as a step toward complete independence. The positive arguments stressed that Confederation would demonstrate to England the willingness of the people of Canada to contribute to their own defence.

The area of relations with the United States is more difficult to assess. For one thing, it is related in a very real way with the economic problems facing the colonies. None the less there are features of the debate which are distinguishably geopolitical in nature and of these the presence of a large and potentially hostile armed force was prominent. This was accompanied by the apprehension that an expansionist America would pursue settlement in the as yet undeveloped northwest.

These geopolitical considerations account in part for the clear and strong elements of anti-Americanism in the value structure of the elite, but it would be an over-simplification to categorize Confederation as primarily an anti-American act. There is in reality evidence of considerable ambivalence in the way the United States is viewed. At the same time as the shortcomings of the American political system and the dangers for Canada inherent in its policies are pointed out, even for one as mistrustful of the United States as John A. Macdonald, the American Constitution and political experience serve as a useful model to perfect the Canadian scheme.[86] His colleague, D'Arcy McGee, noting that the interest of Macdonald in the American Constitution was not of recent date, characterizes the Fathers of Confederation as observers of the American system "who saw its defects as the machine worked and who have prepared contrivances by which it can be improved and kept in more perfect order when applied to ourselves".[87] While a number of speakers refer to other federal systems in summary fashion, no close examination is given to instances other than the American. Another important member of the government, George Brown, recommends the proposed system as "a happy compound of the best features of the British and American Constitutions".[88]

Conclusion

The pragmatic approach inherent in the foregoing statements is characteristic of the debates as a whole. One of the most striking impressions we received from reading the debates was the almost complete absence of any recourse to more than elementary theory in developing a basic constitutional document. Despite the fact that federalism was the most important political idea around which was to pivot the functioning of the entire scheme, the Fathers of Confederation were not federalist by conviction. They did not see federalism, as a basis for the constitution, having any intrinsic value, but simply as the only measure which those who would have preferred either a legislative union or a more narrow federation would accept. We find in the debates no disquisition on the meaning of sovereignty, nor is the language of natural right current money. In effect, a level of thought, the theoretico-practical,[89] is missing in the debates. Accordingly, the arguments of the debators are replete with citations of pertinent examples, both in British experience and elsewhere, the copious use of trade statistics and public accounts, as well as speculation on the probable consequences of various decisions. One is led inescapably to the conclusion that the debates operated against the background of a broad ideological consensus on such crucial matters as responsible government, representative institutions, the monarchical principle, the continued imperial relationship and the nature of public policy.

In light of this type of debate, it is not surprising we find that ideology is not the basis of division between Upper Canadian Reformers and Conservatives, who ostensibly were supposed to have different bases for their political thought.[90] Even among Lower Canadian representatives, whose opposition is of an ideological nature, the interchanges between them in the debates are characterized more by personal vindictiveness and charges of betrayal than by the dissection of their ideological positions. The sole exception arises over the issue of democracy which Conservatives dismiss as mob rule and the Reformers espouse as a principle worthy of vigorous defence.

Perhaps this lack of elevation in the intellectual quality of the debates accounts in part for the less than venerated place that the Fathers of Confederation have achieved in the political culture of Canada when compared to the Founding Fathers of other countries. In essence their work was practical and effective, but not the stuff of national myth-making.

However, a consociational system is not conducive to the creation of "national" myths and heroes.[91] By its very nature it demands the prosaic skills of the compromiser, fixer, or accommodator, and only very rarely does it give the opportunity for leadership that transcends cultural particularism. Thus the high degree of partisanship of the debates themselves created such vitriolic relationships that it was difficult, if not impossible, for the first leaders of the national government to achieve the elevated status that is often accorded to Founding Fathers elsewhere. In addition, the military threat from the United States was in the nature of an apprehended rather than a real invasion, and at any rate was not believed by everyone. Thus, no military hero or group of heroes emerged whose persons and deeds became larger than life. Further, we must recall that the Maritimes were less than willing partners and it was pressure from the Imperial authorities that influenced their final accession to Confederation.

In spite of the lack of the advantages which would have accrued to the country had a complex of unifying national myths emerged from the founding events, the work of the Fathers of Confederation must in the final analysis be judged as a reasonable accommodation among diverse groups with serious problems. If they failed to set in train "nation-building", they certainly were successful in creating a stable "state" system capable of delivering those benefits which citizens seek from government.

APPENDIX

Sample of Parliamentary
Debators

LEGISLATIVE COUNCIL

UC   designates Upper Canada
LC   designates Lower Canada

		CONSTITUENCY
UC	Campbell, A.	Cataraqui
UC	Christie, David	Erie
UC	Currie, James G.	Niagara
LC	Olivier, L. A.	De Lanaudiere
UC	Reesor, David	King's
UC	Ross, John	Life Member
LC	Sanborn, John S.	Wellington
UC	Seymour, Benjamin	Life Member
LC	Taché, E. P.	Life Member
UC	Vidal, A.	St. Clair

LEGISLATIVE ASSEMBLY

UC	Brown, George	South Oxford
UC	Cameron, J. H.	Peel
UC	Cameron, M. C.	North Ontario
LC	Cartier, G. E.	Montreal
LC	Cauchon, J.	Montmorency
LC	Denis, Paul	Beauharnois
LC	Dorion, A. A.	Hochelaga
LC	Dorion, J. B. E.	Drummond and Arthabaska
LC	Dufresene, Joseph	Montcalm
LC	Dunkin, Christopher	Brome
LC	Galt, A. T.	Sherbrooke
LC	Geoffrion, Felix	Vercheres
LC	Harwood, A. Chartiér de Lotbinière	Vaudreuil

UC	Haultain, Frederick W.	Peterborough
LC	Holton, L. H.	Chateauguay
LC	Joly, H. G.	Lotbiniere
LC	Laframboise, Maurice	Bagot
LC	Langevin, H. L.	Dorchester
UC	Macdonald, J. A.	Kingston
UC	Macdonald, J. S.	Cornwall
UC	Mackenzie, A.	Lambton
UC	Mackenzie, Hope	North Oxford
LC	McGee, T. D'Arcy	Montreal West
UC	McGiverin, W.	Lincoln
UC	Morris, Alexander	S. Lanark
LC	O'Halloran, James	Missiquoi
LC	Perrault, Joseph F.	Richelieu
UC	Rankin, Arthur	Essex
LC	Rose, John	Montreal Centre
UC	Shanley, Walter	South Grenville
UC	Scatcherd, Thomas	West Middlesex

Notes

CHAPTER ONE

1. Carl J. Friedrich, *Trends of Federalism in Theory and Practice* (New York: Frederick A. Praeger, 1968), see p. 27 and p. 119.
2. A number of quite defensible reasons account for this. Most prominent are the inevitable focus on the central authority during the period of the two great wars, as well as the tremendous responsibility that fell on the federal government at the time of the Great Depression and continued with the development and expansion of the welfare state.
3. See in particular, Kenneth D. MacRae, ed., *Consociational Democracy: Political Accommodation in Segmented Societies* (Toronto: McClelland and Stewart, 1974) and Ivo D. Duchacek, *Comparative Federalism: The Territorial Dimension in Politics* (New York: Holt, Rinehart, and Winston, 1970).
4. Alan C. Cairns, "Alternative Styles in the Study of Canadian Politics", *Canadian Journal of Political Science*, Vol. VII (March, 1974), p. 116.
5. Barrington Moore Jr., *Social Origins of Dictatorship and Democracy: Lord and Peasant in the Making of the Modern World* (Boston: Beacon Press, 1966).
6. Louis Hartz, *The Founding of New Societies: Studies in the History of the United States, Latin America, South Africa, Canada, and Australia* (New York: Harcourt, Brace and World, 1964).
7. For an interesting discussion of this subject, see Robert V. Edington, "The Ancient Idea of Founding and the Contemporary Study of Political Change", *Polity*, Vol. VII (Winter 1974), pp. 163-179.
8. The most prominent include, J. M. S. Careless, *Brown of the Globe*, 2 vols. (Toronto: Macmillan, 1959, 1963); Donald G. Creighton, *John A. Macdonald*, 2 vols. (Toronto: Macmillan, 1952, 1955); Isabel Skelton, *The Life and Times of Thomas D'Arcy McGee* (Gardenvale: Garden City Press, 1925); O. D. Skelton, *The Life and Times of Sir Alexander Tilloch Galt* (Toronto: Oxford University Press, 1920); Dale C. Thomson, *Alexander Mackenzie, Clear Grit* (Toronto: Macmillan, 1960); Bruce W. Hodgins, *John Sandfield Macdonald* (Toronto: University of Toronto Press, 1971); and Andrée Desilets, *Hector-Louis Langevin: un père de la Confédération Canadienne 1826-1906* (Quebec: Les Presses de L'Université Laval, 1969).
9. An obvious exception to this comment is William Ormsby's excellent study, *The Emergence of the Federal Concept in Canada, 1839-1845* (Toronto: University of Toronto Press, 1969).
10. K. C. Wheare, *Federal Government* (London: Oxford University Press, 1953).
11. R. L. Watts, *New Federations: Experiments in the Commonwealth* (Oxford: Clarendon Press, 1966).
12. R. MacGregor Dawson, *The Government of Canada* (Toronto: University of Toronto Press, 1947).
13. J. S. Mallory, *The Structure of*

Canadian Government (Toronto: Macmillan, 1971).

14. W. S. Livingston, "A Note on the Nature of Federalism", in J. Peter Meekison, ed., *Canadian Federalism: Myth or Reality?*, 2nd ed. (Toronto: Methuen, 1971), pp. 19-30.

15. Michael Stein, "Federal Political Systems and Federal Societies", in ibid., p. 42.

16. Arend Lijphart, "Consociational Democracy", *World Politics*, Vol. XXI (Jan. 1969), pp. 207-225; and "Cultural Diversity and Theories of Political Integration", *Canadian Journal of Political Science*, Vol. IV (March, 1971), pp. 1-14.

17. S. J. R. Noel, "Consociational Democracy and Canadian Federalism", *Canadian Journal of Political Science*, Vol. IV (March 1971), pp. 15-18.

18. McRae, *Consociational Democracy*, pp. 238-268.

19. William Riker, *Federalism: Origin, Operation, Significance* (Boston: Little, Brown and Co., 1964), pp. 12.

20. Ibid., pp. 129-135.

21. E. R. Black, "Federal Strains within a Canadian Party", *The Dalhousie Review*, Vol. XLV (Fall 1965), pp. 307-323.

22. Alan C. Cairns, "The Electoral System and the Party System in Canada", *Canadian Journal of Political Science*, Vol. I (March, 1968), pp. 55-80.

23. Denis Smith, "Prairie Revolt, Federalism and the Party System", in Hugh G. Thorburn, ed., *Party Politics in Canada*, 2nd ed. (Scarborough: Prentice-Hall, 1967).

24. F. C. Engelmann and M. A. Schwartz, *Political Parties and the Canadian Social Structure* (Scarborough: Prentice-Hall, 1967).

25. E. R. Black and Alan C. Cairns, "A Different Perspective on Canadian Federalism", in J. Peter Meekison, ed., *Canadian Federalism: Myth or Reality?*, 1st ed. (Toronto: Methuen, 1968), pp. 81-97.

26. Edwin R. Black, *Divided Loyalties: Canadian Concepts of Federalism* (Montreal: McGill-Queen's University Press, 1975).

27. D. V. Smiley, *Canada in Question:* *Federalism in the Seventies*, 2nd ed. (Toronto: McGraw-Hill Ryerson, 1976).

28. Ibid., p. 107.

29. Edgar Gallant, "The Machinery of Federal-Provincial Relations; I", and R. M. Burns, "The Machinery of Federal-Provincial Relations: II", in Meekison, *Canadian Federalism*, 1st. ed., pp. 287-297 and pp. 298-304.

30. Richard Simeon, *Federal Provincial Diplomacy: The Making of Recent Policy in Canada* (Toronto: University of Toronto Press, 1972).

CHAPTER TWO

1. See in particular, W. L. Morton, *The Critical Years: The Union of British North America, 1857–1873* (Toronto: McClelland and Stewart, 1968); Donald Creighton, *The Road to Confederation: The Emergence of Canada 1863–1867* (Toronto: Macmillan, 1964); and P. B. Waite, *The Life and Times of Confederation 1864–1867: Politics, Newspapers and the Union of British North America* (Toronto: University of Toronto Press, 1962), for an overview of the Confederation period.

2. *Parliamentary Debates on the Subject of the Confederation of the British North American Provinces* (Quebec: Hunter and Rose and Co., 1865). Hereinafter referred to as *Debates*. Arguments stressing the importance of the Province of Canada in the decision-making process leading to Confederation are many. For example, P. B. Waite believes that Confederation was pushed jointly by Canada and the British Colonial office, and that the Maritime Provinces were dragged in kicking and screaming. See his *Life and Times of Confederation*, pp. 4–5. See also, William M. Whitelaw, *The Maritimes and Canada before Confederation* (Toronto: Oxford University Press, 1934).

3. Harold and Margaret Sprout, "Environmental Factors in the Study of International Politics", *Journal of Conflict Resolution*, Vol. I (1957), p. 322.

4. Michael Brecher, Blema Steinberg,

and Janice Stein, "A Framework for Research on Foreign Policy Behaviour", *Journal of Conflict Resolution*, Vol. XIII (1969), pp. 75–101.

5. For the original model, see ibid, p. 80.

6. Donald R. Matthews, *The Social Background of Political Decision-makers* (New York: Random House, 1954), p. 2.

7. In order to compile this information, we consulted the standard biographical sources: the *Canadian Parliamentary Companion*; the *Canadian Directory of Parliament*; the *Dominion Annual Register*; J. C. Dent, ed., *Canadian Portrait Gallery*, 4 vols. (Toronto: J. B. Magwin, 1880–1881); M. O. Hammond *Confederation and Its Leaders* (New York: George H. Doran, 1917); Marc La Terreur, ed., *Dictionary of Canadian Biography*, Vol. X (Toronto: University of Toronto Press, 1972); Francess G. Halpenny, ed., *Dictionary of Canadian Biography*, Vol. IX (Toronto: University of Toronto Press, 1976); Henry J. Morgan, *Sketches of Celebrated Canadians and Persons Connected with Canada* (Montreal: R. Worthington, 1865); George M. Rose, *A Cyclopaedia of Canadian Biography* (Toronto: Rose Publishing Co., 1886); and W. Stewart Wallace, ed., *The Macmillan Dictionary of Canadian Biography* (Toronto: Macmillan, 1955, 1963). We also visited the Public Archives of Canada, the National Library, and the Library of Parliament as well as the editorial offices of the Dictionary of Canadian Biography and the Hiram Walker Historical Museum.

8. Alexander L. George, "The 'Operational Code': A Neglected Approach to the Study of Political Leaders and Decision-making", *International Studies Quarterly*, Vol. XII (1969), pp. 190–222.

9. David S. McLellan, "The 'Operational Code' Approach to the Study of Political Leaders: Dean Acheson's Philosophical and Instrumental Beliefs", *Canadian Journal of Political Science*, Vol. IV (1971), pp. 52–75.

10. Ole Holsti, "The 'Operational Code' Approach to the Study of Political Leaders; John Foster Dulles' Philosophical and Instrumental Beliefs", *Canadian Journal of Political Science*, Vol. III (1970), pp. 123–157.

11. Donald Arthur Lawrence, "The 'Operational Code' of Lester B. Pearson", paper presented to the Annual Meeting of the Canadian Political Science Association, University of Toronto 3–6 June, 1974.

12. Louis Hartz, *The Founding of New Societies: Studies in the History of the United States, Latin America, South Africa, Canada, and Australia* (New York: Harcourt, Brace and World, 1964), pp. 33–40.

13. Ibid., pp. 26–33.

14. Comments on a theme that were concluded in less than a full sentence on the following column were not coded for the second column.

15. Ole R. Holsti, *Content Analysis for the Social Sciences and Humanities* (Don Mills: Addison-Wesley, 1969), p. 140. In the formula $M =$ the number of coding decisions on which two specific teams are in agreement, while N_1 and $N_2 =$ the number of coding decisions made by each team independently.

16. Most discrepancies in coding did not stem from miscoding, that is, one team coding the same comment as a political theme while the other coded it as an economic theme. Rather our problem involved one or the other team failing to recognize the presence of a particular theme. Reading the *Debates* aloud increased our coefficients of reliability considerably.

17. Bertrand de Jouvenal, *The Pure Theory of Politics* (New Haven: Yale University Press, 1963), p. 207.

18. Ibid.,

19. Donald V. Smiley, *Canada in Question: Federalism in the Seventies*, 2nd ed. (Toronto:

McGraw-Hill, Ryerson, 1976), pp. 184–199.

CHAPTER THREE

1. Alan C. Cairns, "Alternative Styles in the Study of Canadian Politics", *Canadian Journal of Political Science*, Vol. VII (March, 1974), p. 115.

2. See for example, Frank H. Underhill, *The Image of Confederation* (Toronto: Hunter Rose and Co., 1974), especially Chapters 1, 3, 4, and 5.

3. Fernand Ouellet, *Histoire économique et sociale du Québec* (Montreal: Fides, 1966).

4. For instance, the conflict between the Swiss liberals in Bern and the Roman Catholic cantons had led to a civil war in 1847, the defeat of the secessionists, the revision of the Helvitic confederation turning Switzerland into a federal state, and the expulsion of the Jesuits as fomentors of secession. The attitudes of the liberals in Switzerland were not peculiar to them, but were typical of the representatives of European liberalism.

5. For one example, see the chapter entitled "La Confédération et les minorités", in Lionel Groulx, *La Confédération Canadienne* (Montreal: Le Devoir, 1913).

6. Ramsay Cook, *Canada and the French-Canadian Question (Toronto: Macmillan, 1966), p. 146.*

7. For a contemporary discussion of the sociological conception of Quebec see F. Dumont, *La Vigile du Québec* (Montreal: Hurtubise, 1971).

8. P. E. Trudeau, "Some Obstacles to Democracy in Quebec", in Mason Wade, ed., *Canadian Dualism/La Dualité Canadienne* (Toronto: University of Toronto and Presses Universitaires, Laval, 1960).

9. Here is a prime example of this confusion: "The French [Canadians] wanted control over the colonial parliament to protect the collective interests of French Canadians. This goal was often in direct conflict with the individual liberties of English Canadians. For example, the French

majority in the assembly of Lower Canada obstructed efforts by English Canadians to further economic development, which was sent at the time as a pre-eminently liberal endeavour". W. Christian and C. Campbell, *Political Parties and Ideologies in Canada* (Toronto: McGraw-Hill Ryerson, 1974), p. 34.

10. Louis Hartz, *The Founding of New Societies: Studies of History of the United States, Latin America, South Africa, Canada and Australia* (New York: Harcourt, Brace and World, 1964), pp. 3–65.

11. Ouellet, *Histoire économique et sociale*, p. 466. We refer to the attitudes in the 1840s, but one must not lose sight of Ouellet's contention that Papineau attempted to preserve traditional institutions. In his latter study of the period, Ouellet says that Papineau "was dedicated to the defence of the seigniorial regime" (p. 508) as well as "the *Coutume de Paris* and, probably the tithe" (p. 510). Hence he concludes that under his leadership, "the Patriote movement in the final analysis remained a nationalist and conservative movement". (p. 511). *Le Bas Canada, 1791–1840* (Ottawa: Editions de l'Université d'Ottawa, 1976).

12. We refer particularly to the political alliance, short lived though it may have been, between liberals from Lower Canada and liberals from Upper Canada during the Brown-Dorion Administration. However, Marcel Rioux has pointed out the conflict between this new bourgeoisie and the merchant class of Lower Canada. "A new Francophone bourgeoisie, made up of people from the liberal professions, was to oppose the mercantile class, which in turn, was to represent the Anglophone minority". Marcel Rioux, "The Development of Ideologies in Quebec", in O. M. Kruhlak, R. Schultz, and S. I. Pobihushchy, eds., *The Canadian Political Process: A Reader*, rev. ed. (Toronto: Holt, Rinehart, and Winston, 1973), p. 69.

On more detailed aspects of social stratification in Lower Canada before Confederation, see Robert Rumilly, *Histoire de la Province de Québec*, Vol. I (Montreal: Editions Bernard Valiquette, 1940).

13. J. M. S. Careless, *The Union of the Canadas: The Growth of Canadian Institutions, 1841–1857* (Toronto: McClelland and Stewart, 1967), p. 165.

14. R. MacGregor Dawson, *The Government of Canada*, 4th ed., rev. by Norman Ward (Toronto: University of Toronto Press, 1963), p. 23.

15. J. C. L. Durham, *The Report of the Earl of Durham* (London: Metheun, 1905), p. 113. Hereinafter referred to as *The Durham Report*.

16. Ramsay Cook, with John C. Ricker, and John T. Saywell, *Canada, A Modern Study* (Toronto: Clarke, Irwin and Company, 1967), p. 52.

17. Ged Martin, *The Durham Report and British Policy* (Cambridge: Cambridge University Press, 1972), p. 17.

18. Ibid., p. 5.

19. Cook et al. *Canada*, p. 51

20. Ibid.

21. Ibid., p. 52.

22. Chester New, *Lord Durham* (London: Dawsons of Pall Mall, 1968), pp. 497–499.

23. *The Durham Report*, p. 23.

24. Ibid., p. 29.

25. Ibid., p. 22.

26. Alexis de Tocqueville had high praise for local government in England, which he visited in 1833 for the first time. For details, see Seymour Drescher, *Tocqueville and England* (Cambridge: Harvard University Press, 1964), pp. 43–4; pp. 79–84; pp. 91–95; pp. 101–102; p. 191, and p. 204.

27. J. S. Mill, *Considerations on Representative Government* (Chicago: Gateway-Regnery, 1962), p. 346.

28. *The Durham Report*, p. 18. De Tocqueville said that "the spirit of equality and democracy is alive there as in the United States . . . ". *Journey to America* (New Haven: Yale, 1959), p. 190. The main difference between Durham and de

Tocqueville on this point is that de Tocqueville viewed this situation favourably and Durham saw it as an effect of underdevelopment.

29. *The Durham Report*, p. 195.

30. Ibid., p. 214.

31. De Tocqueville, *Journey to America*, pp. 34–47. De Tocqueville visited Canada in 1831.

32. *The Durham Report*, p. 218

33. Ibid., p. 212.

34. Ibid., p. 225.

35. Leo Strauss maintained that liberals set as their goal the universal and homogeneous state. For this reason, they are less tolerant than conservatives of linguistic diversity and variations in folkways. See, *Liberalism, Ancient and Modern* (New York: Basic Books, 1968), especially pp. v-vi.

36. *The Durham Report* p. 211.

37. Donald Creighton, *Dominion of the North* (Toronto: Macmillan, 1962), p. 247.

38. Paul G. Cornell, *The Alignment of Political Groups in Canada: 1841–1867* (Toronto: University of Toronto Press, 1962), pp. 67–68

39. Ibid., p. 62.

40. Jean-Paul Bernard, *Les Rouges: Libéralisme, Nationalisme et Anticléricalisme au milieu du XIXe siècle* (Montreal: Les Presses de l'Université du Québec, 1971), p. 1.

41. Careless, *Union of the Canadas*, pp. 161–165.

42. Ibid., pp. 119–120

43. Bernard, *Les Rouges*, p. 3.

44. Careless, *Union of the Canadas*, p. 4.

45. Ibid., p. 182.

46. Frank H. Underhill, "Some Aspects of Upper Canadian Radical Opinion in the Decade Before Confederation", *Canadian Historical Association Report* (1927), pp. 46–61.

47. G. F. G. Stanley, "Act or Pact? Another Look at Confederation", *Canadian Historical Association Report* (1956) pp. 1–25; see also Morton, *The Critical Years*, p. 10.

48. Waite, *Life and Times of Confederation, 1864–1867: Politics, Newspapers, and the Union of British North America* (Toronto: University of Toronto Press, 1962), p. 37.

49. Ibid., pp. 37–38
50. G. W. Brown, "The Grit Party and the Great Reform Convention of 1859", *Canadian Historical Review*, Vol. XVI (September 1935), pp. 245–265; see also J. M. S. Careless, "The Toronto Globe and Agrarian Radicalism", *Canadian Historical Review*, Vol. XXIX (March 1948), pp. 14–39.
51. Morton, *The Critical Years*, p. 15.
52. Cornell, *The Alignment of Political Groups*, p. 57.
53. Donald V. Smiley, ed., *The Rowell-Sirois Report: Book I (Toronto: McClelland and Stewart, 1964), p. 14.
54. A. W. Currie, *Canadian Economic Development*, rev. ed. (Toronto: Thomas Nelson and Sons, 1951), p. 688.
55. Gary Teeple, "Land, labour and capital in pre-Confederation Canada", in Gary Teeple, ed., *Capitalism and the National Question in Canada* (Toronto: University of Toronto Press, 1972), p. 58.
56. Smiley, ed., *The Rowell-Sirois Report*, p. 15. See also R. Cole Harris and John Warkentin, *Canada Before Confederation: A Study in Historical Geography* (New York: Oxford University Press, 1974), pp. 135–142.
57. A. R. M. Lower, "The Trade in Square Timber", in W. T. Easterbrook and M. H. Watkins, eds., *Approaches to Canadian Economic History* (Toronto: McClelland and Stewart, 1967), pp. 28–48.
58. Currie, *Canadian Economic Development*, p. 78.
59. Lower, "Trade in Square Timber", pp. 46–48
60. Leo A. Johnson, *History of the County of Ontario* (Whitby, Ontario: The Corporation of the County of Ontario, 1973), p. 212.
61. Currie, *Canadian Economic Development*, p. 81.
62. Ibid., p. 82.
63. Donald G. Creighton, *The Commercial Empire of the St. Lawrence, 1760–1850* (Toronto: Ryerson Press, 1937); see also J. M. S. Careless, "The Toronto Globe and Agrarian Radicalism", *Canadian

Historical Review, Vol. XXIX, (March 1948), pp. 14–39.
64. Smiley, ed., *The Rowell-Sirois Report*, p. 218, fn. 43.
65. Robin W. Winks, *Canada and the United States: The Civil War Years* (Baltimore: John Hopkins Press, 1971), pp. 337–360.
66. D. C. Thomson and R. F. Swanson, *Canadian Foreign Policy: Options and Perspectives* (Toronto: McGraw-Hill Ryerson, 1971).
67. For views indicating an initial pro-Northern stance, see Helen G. MacDonald, *Canadian Public Opinion on the American Civil War* (New York: Columbia University Press, 1926); and Fred Landon, "Canadian Opinion of Southern Secession, 1860–61", *Canadian Historical Review*, Vol. I, (Sept. 1920), pp. 255–266. A later scholar, Robin Winks, is far less certain of the degree of pro-Northern sentiment. See chapter 2 of his *Canada and the United States*.
68. Winks, *Canada and the United States*, pp. 52–53.
69. Ibid., pp. 69–72.
70. C. P. Stacey, "Britain's Withdrawal from North America, 1864–1871", *Canadian Historical Review*, Vol. XXXVI (Sept. 1955) p. 186.
71. Waite, *Life and Times of Confederation*, p. 19.
72. Morton, *Critical Years*, pp. 60–70.
73. P. B. Waite, *Confederation, 1854–1867* (Toronto: Holt, Rinehart and Winston, 1972), p. 18.
74. Winks, *Canada and the United States*, pp. 295–336.
75. Ibid., p. 317.
76. C. P. Stacey, "Fenianism and the Rise of National Feeling in Canada at the Time of Confederation", *Canadian Historical Review*, Vol. XII (September, 1931), pp. 233–261.
77. A. G. Doughty, "The Awakening of Canadian Interest in the Northwest", *Report of the Annual Meeting of the Canadian Historical Association, 1928*, pp. 5–11.
78. Careless, *Union of the Canadas*, p. 205.
79. Winks, *Canada and the United States*, p. 4.
80. D. G. Creighton, "The United States

and Canadian Confederation",
Canadian Historical Review, Vol.
xxxix (Sept. 1958), pp. 215–219.

81. Ibid., p. 222. For another assessment
of the impact of the external
environment on Confederation, see
C. P. Stacey, "Confederation: The
Atmosphere of Crisis", in *Profiles of
a Province: Studies in the History of
Ontario* (Toronto: Ontario Historical
Society, 1967), pp. 73–79. See also
the studies on the investigation of
public opinion in Canada
concerning the United States in the
last century by S. F. Wise and
Robert Craig Brown, *Canada Views
the United States, Nineteenth
Century Political Attitudes* (Toronto:
Macmillan, 1967).

CHAPTER FOUR

1. Lewis J. Edinger and Donald D.
Searing, "Social Background in Elite
Analysis: A Methodological
Inquiry", *American Political Science
Review*, Vol LVI, (June 1967), pp. 428
–445; and Donald D. Searing, "The
Comparative Study of Elite
Socialization", *Comparative Political
Studies*, Vol. I (1969), pp. 471–500.

2. Edinger and Searing, "Social
Background", p. 436.

3. Searing, "The Comparative Study",
pp. 478–479.

4. Though it is difficult to transpose
terms such as "urban" and "rural"
back over one hundred years, we
believe our criteria accurately reflect
what was essentially urban and rural
in the context of Canadian society in
the 1860s. The following census data
indicate the size of a number of
urban and urban-rural mixed areas
as of 1861: Montreal–90,322,
Quebec–59,990, Toronto–44,821,
Hamilton–19,096, Ottawa–14,669,
London–11,555, Kingston–13,743,
Brantford–6,251, St. Catharines–
6,284, Trois Rivières–6,058,
Belleville–6,277, Lévis–5,333,
Chatham–4,466, and Sorel–4,778.
Census of Canada (1870) Vol. I
(Ottawa: I. B. Taylor, 1873), p. 428.

5. We estimate, on the basis of census
data, that the percentage of the
population living in urban areas (i.e.,
those living in cities with a
population over ten thousand in
1865) was no greater than 10 per
cent.

6. The basic alignment in the 8th
Parliament (1863–64) was nearly
equally divided between Reformers
and Conservatives. See Paul G.
Cornell, *The Alignment of Political
Groups in Canada: 1841–1867*
(Toronto: University of Toronto
Press, 1962), Table 18, p. 110.
Because we tapped the ethnicity
dimension on a number of other
variables, our coding of party
affiliation does not include a
breakdown of Reformers and
Conservatives in Lower Canada by
ethnic group. Therefore such
English-speaking Lower Canadian
representatives as Luther Holton are
coded with French Canadians such
as the Dorion brothers. Likewise,
English-speaking Lower Canadian
representatives such as Alexander
Galt and Christopher Dunkin are
classified as Conservatives along
with George Cartier and Hector
Langevin.

7. Ibid., p. 85.

8. See in particular, Richard E.
Dawson and Kenneth Prewitt
Political Socialization (Boston: Little
Brown, 1969); Jack Dennis,
Socialization to Politics (New York:
John Wiley, 1971); Robert D. Hess
and Judith V. Torney, *The
Development of Political Attitudes in
Children* (Chicago: Aldine, 1967);
David Easton and Jack Dennis,
Children in the Political System
(New York: McGraw-Hill, 1969);
and David Easton and Robert Hess,
"The Child's Political World",
Midwest Journal of Political Science,
Vol. VI (August, 1962), pp. 229-246.

9. Based on the census of 1870, we
estimate that no more than 11 per
cent of the population comprised the
"professional" and "commercial"
classes, while in our sample, fully
82.9 per cent are classified
"professional" or "commercial", see
Census of Canada (1870) Vol. II, p.
345.

10. Alfred Dubuc describes the passing
of control of the legislative assembly
"from the hands of both the

seigneurs and the merchant traders into the hands of the rising middle class of professional men and small local merchants" in the period before Confederation. "Problems in the Study of the Stratification of the Canadian Society from 1760 to 1840", in Michiel Horn and Ronald Sabourin, eds., *Studies in Canadian Social History* (Toronto: McClelland and Stewart, 1974), p. 133. Robert Rumilly, on the other hand, referring particularly to Lower Canada, says that during the Confederation period itself, the largest part of the bourgeoisie was made up of lawyers, notaries and doctors, and that this class was made up of the children of gentlemen farmers. They can also be seen as spokesmen for agricultural interests. Robert Rumilly, *Histoire de la Province de Québec*, Vol. I, (Montreal: Editions Bernard Valiquette, 1940).

11. Dubuc has argued that the cleavage between groups in earlier Canadian society has been heretofore examined primarily in regard to ethnic differences and not sufficiently according to social stratification which he deems to be ordinarily of greater significance. He argues that the development of Canadian society in the first half of the nineteenth century saw an old aristocracy replaced by a new, financial, aristocracy. In time as commercial capitalism was replaced by industrial capitalism, conflicts arose between merchant traders and landowners, on one hand, and industrial entrepreneurs, on the other; the former in favour of protection, the latter of free trade. In the light of this interpretation, he maintains that "the rising of the new middle class, opposed to the great bourgeoisie of the merchant traders, provoked the rebellion of 1837 both in Upper and Lower Canada". Dubuc, "Problems in the Studies of Stratification", p. 128.

12. For a fascinating and detailed account of the social changes which occurred in Upper Canada in the period immediately prior to

Confederation, see Leo A. Johnson, *History of the County of Ontario* (Whitby, Ontario: The Corporation of the County of Ontario, 1973), Chapters 11, 12, 13, and 14.

13. Louis Hartz, *The Founding of New Societies: Studies in the History of the United States, Latin America, South Africa, Canada, and Australia* (New York: Harcourt, Brace and World, 1964), Chapters 1, 2, and 3.

CHAPTER FIVE

1. Michael Brecher, Blema Steinberg, and Janice Stein, "A Framework for Research on Foreign Policy Behaviour," *Journal of Conflict Resolution*, Vol. XII (1969) pp. 89.

2. *Parliamentary Debates on the Subject of the Confederation of the British North American Provinces* (Quebec: Hunter and Rose and Co., 1865, pp. 585–626.)

3. Ibid., p. 61.

4. Ibid., p. 833.

5. Ibid., pp. 925-6.

6. Ibid., p. 795.

7. Ibid., pp. 396–397.

8. Ibid., p. 57 and p. 60.

9. Ibid., "I propose the adoption of the rainbow as our emblem. By the endless variety of its tints the rainbow will give an excellent idea of the diversity of races, religions, sentiments and interests of the different parts of the Confederation. By its slender and elongated form, the rainbow would afford a perfect representation of the geographical configuration of the Confederation. By its lack of consistence—an image without substance—the rainbow would represent aptly the solidity of our Confederation." p. 354. Do we not have in this debate an anticipation of Lijpart's theory of consociational democracy?

10. Ibid., p. 57, pp. 59–62.

11. Ibid., pp. 166–167.

12. Ibid., pp. 970–973.

13. Ibid., pp. 586–592.

14. Ibid., p. 358.

15. Ibid., pp. 84–115.

16. Ibid., p. 676.

17. Ibid., see Perrault, pp. 591–596; Dorion, pp. 245–253; and Joly, pp. 457–458.

18. Ibid., see Scatcherd, p. 748 and 756 and M. C. Cameron, p. 451–452.
19. Ibid., p. 921.
20. Ibid., see Brown, pp. 103–104;and McGivern, pp. 467–470.
21. Ibid., see Brown, pp. 100–102; Cartier, p. 55; and J. H. Cameron, pp. 965–966.
22. Ibid., see McGee, pp. 138–139.
23. Ibid., see Taché, pp. 6–7 and 343–344; Brown, pp. 104–106; H. Mackenzie, p. 680., J. H. Cameron, pp. 964–965; and Rankin, pp. 916–917.
24. Ibid., see Ross, pp. 76–80; and Galt, pp. 63–71.
25. Ibid., see Rankin, pp. 919–922.
26. Ibid., see M. C. Cameron, p. 453; and Dunkin, p. 523.
27. Those whose feelings ran especially strongly on this issue included J. H. Cameron, John Sanborn, Benjamin Seymour, and Alexander Vidal.
28. Debates, see Morris, pp. 434–437.
29. Ibid., see Christie, pp. 217–221; and McGivern, pp. 471–472.
30. Ibid., see Campbell, pp. 20–24; and J. A. MacDonald, pp. 36–37.
31. Ibid., see M. C. Cameron, pp. 451–452; A. A. Dorion, p. 252, p. 868.
32. Ibid., see Reesor, p. 329; J. H. Cameron, pp. 962–965; and Vidal, pp. 301–306.
33. Ibid., see Taché, p. 240.
34. Ibid., see Campbell, pp. 22–24; and J. A. MacDonald, pp. 35–38.
35. Ibid., p. 434.
36. Ibid., p. 503.
37. Ibid., see Olivier, p. 176; and Laframboise, pp. 850–852.
38. Ibid., pp. 29–33.
39. Ibid., see Langevin, p. 373; and Cartier, pp. 60–61.
40. Ibid., pp. 690–692.
41. Ibid., p. 860.
42. Ibid., pp. 793–795.
43. Ibid., p. 50.
44. Ibid., see Seymour, p. 200; and A. A. Dorion, p. 253.
45. Ibid., p. 293.
46. Ibid., p. 680.
47. Ibid., p. 47.
48. Ibid., p. 162.
49. Ibid., see Vidal, p. 302; and Seymour, p. 206.
50. Ibid., pp. 290–291.
51. Ibid., see J. A. Macdonald, p. 26, pp. 31–32; Cartier, pp. 53–54; and Brown, p. 102, p. 114.
52. For example, Currie, Reesor, and Olivier.
53. For example, Vidal and Sanborn.
54. Debates, p. 290.
55. Ibid., p. 962. Cameron voted in favour of Confederation.
56. Ibid., p. 296.
57. Ibid., p. 31.
58. In the words of McGee: "And that there shall be no doubt about our position in regard to that document we say, question it you may, or accept it you may, but alter it you may not."
59. Debates, p. 328.
60. Ibid., pp. 63-64.
61. Ibid., pp. 64. See also the argument of George Cartier, p. 60.
62. Ibid., p. 65.
63. Ibid., p. 471.
64. Ibid., pp. 831–832.
65. Ibid., p. 862.
66. Ibid., p. 863.
67. Ibid., p. 451.
68. Ibid., p. 77.
69. Ibid., p. 966.
70. Ibid., p. 413.
71. Ibid., p. 414.
72. Ibid., pp. 636–637.
73. Ibid., p. 431.
74. Ibid., p. 251.
75. Ibid., p. 257.
76. Ibid., p. 752.
77. Ibid., p. 759.
78. Ibid.
79. Ibid., p. 49.
80. Ibid., p. 52.
81. Ibid., p. 164.
82. Ibid., p. 979.
83. Ibid., p. 65.
84. Ibid., p. 66.
85. Ibid.
86. Ibid., p. 366.
87. Ibid., p. 377.
88. Ibid.
89. Ibid., p. 378.
90. Ibid., p. 429.
91. Ibid., p. 676.
92. Ibid., p. 879.
93. Ibid., p. 259.
94. Ibid., p. 260.
95. Ibid., p. 267.
96. Ibid., p. 859.
97. Ibid., p. 861.
98. Ibid.

99. Ibid., p. 755.
100. Ibid., p. 757.
101. Ibid., p. 272.
102. Ibid., pp. 129–130.
103. Ibid., p. 130.
104. Ibid., pp. 133–134.
105. Ibid., p. 395.
106. Ibid., p. 398.
107. Ibid.
108. Ibid., p. 828.
109. Ibid., pp. 964–965.
110. Ibid., p. 342.
111. Ibid., pp. 342–343.
112. Ibid., p. 203; see also remarks on p. 299.
113. Ibid., p. 708.
114. Ibid., p. 862.
115. Ibid., p. 868.
116. Ibid.
117. Ibid., p. 869.
118. Ibid., p. 256.
119. Ibid.
120. Ibid., p. 257.
121. Ibid., p. 343.
122. Ibid., p. 55.
123. Ibid., p. 56. See also the argument of Paul Denis on p. 873.
124. Ibid., p. 143.
125. Ibid.
126. Ibid., p. 869.
127. Ibid., p. 871.
128. Ibid., p. 625. Claims Perrault, "Our people will have learned that of two evils they must choose the least, and that on a comparison between Confederation and annexation, the least evil will not, unfortunately, be found to be Confederation."
129. Ibid., p. 293.
130. Ibid., p. 296.
131. Ibid., pp. 438–439.
132. Ibid., pp. 631–632.
133. Ibid., p. 634.
134. Ibid., p. 966.
135. Ibid., p. 968.
136. Ibid., p. 532.
137. Ibid., p. 449.
138. Ibid., p. 204.
139. Ibid. See in particular the comments of George Brown, pp. 86, 98, and 103-104. Brown maintains that western development is one of the highest priorities of Confederation.
140. Ibid., p. 467.
141. Ibid., p. 469.
142. Ibid., p. 433.
143. Ibid., p. 443.
144. Ibid., p. 444.
145. Ibid., p. 750.
146. Ibid., for Cameron's comments see p. 452; for Rankin's p. 917.
147. Ibid., p. 522.

CHAPTER SIX

1. In contrast, the total vote in favour of Confederation in the Council was 75 per cent, and in the Assembly it was 73.3 per cent. Our elite, therefore contains a greater percentage of opponents to Confederation than was found in Parliament as a whole.
2. See Chapter 4, pp. 45-46.
3. Pertinent to this point, J.M.S. Careless points out in his article, "The Toronto Globe and Agrarian Radicalism, 1850–67", that the *Globe* represented urban liberalism not agrarian democracy. According to Careless' analysis, it spoke for the western business community centred in a growing Toronto. *Canadian Historical Review*, Vol. xxix (March 1948), pp. 14–39.
4. Of the entire government, twelve in total, only one, William McDougall, was born in Upper Canada.
5. Of those who had immigrated from the British Isles only James O'Halloran voted in opposition to Confederation. We can assume, however, that Christopher Dunkin, had he voted, would also have opposed the scheme.
6. Summary statistics measuring levels of association present special problems working with a small sample. Chi-Square and related statistics such as Cramer's V and Contingency Coefficient, the most popular statistics for indicating the strength of relationships between nominal level independent and dependent variables, are unreliable because of the number of expected cell frequencies below five. While the percentagized tables which we have presented give an accurate visual portrayal of the very definite directions of the data, we include the results of a multiple classification analysis which examines the singular and joint impact of party affiliation and country of birth on the

dependent variable, the vote on Confederation. Eta-square, interpreted as the proportion of total variance in the dependent variable explained by each independent alone is 0.54 for party affiliation and 0.37 for country of birth. The multiple R^2 for both independent variables, (i.e., total variance explained), is 0.85.

7. For example, Frank Underhill decries generally the lack of learned and elevated discussion about questions in the political realm, not only at Confederation, but in Canadian history generally. Specifically, with regard to Confederation, he remarks that "later Canadians have had to reflect that the 'new nationality' was very imperfectly based upon any deep popular feeling". "Some Reflections on the Liberal Tradition in Canada", *Approaches to Canadian History*, Ramsay Cook, R. Craig Brown, and Carl Berger, eds. (Toronto: University of Toronto Press, 1967), p. 38.

CHAPTER SEVEN

1. If there is any qualification to be made to this statement, it would concern members of the *rouge* party, who were accused of insincerity in their defence of French-Canadian cultural values when they had once sought a secular school system. Of course it may be that their earlier secularism might have been modified by the time of the Debates. For a discussion of this facet of Lower Canadian liberalism, see Jean-Paul Bernard, *Les Rouges, Libéralisme, Nationalisme et Anticléricalisme au milieu du XIXe siècle* (Montreal, Les Presses de l'Universite du Québec, 1971) p. 109, p. 122 and p. 166.

2. Seymour Martin Lipset, *Political Man: The Social Bases of Politics* (Garden City: Doubleday and Co., 1966), p. 71.

3. Donald V. Smiley, *Canada in Question: Federalism in the Seventies*, 2nd ed. (Toronto: McGraw-Hill Ryerson, 1976), p. 184.

4. In *The First New Nation*, Seymour Martin Lipset gives formal recognition to the importance of "key historical events" in the formation of national value systems. (Garden City: Doubleday and Co., 1967), pp. 7-8. See also David V. J. Bell, "Methodological Problems in the Study of Canadian Political Culture", paper presented at the 1974 meeting of the Canadian Political Science Association.

5. For a study which gives a sympathetic appraisal of confederalism as a system of government, see A. R. Kear, "Confederalism: A New Theory of the Principles and Practices of Confederations", paper presented to the 1976 meeting of the Canadian Political Science Association.

6. It was not only that the Fathers of Confederation expected any amendments would be passed by the British Parliament on request of the Canadian authorities, but also that they realized the difficulty of achieving an amendment process within the context of the Quebec Resolutions which convinced them to avoid a confrontation of this issue. A method of amendment acceptable to all parties continues to elude political leaders in the 1970s.

7. On this point, see W. M. Whitelaw, *The Quebec Conference* Historical Booklet No. 20 (Ottawa: Canadian Historical Association, 1966), p. 16.

8. John Stuart Mill, *Considerations on Representative Government* (Chicago: Henry Regnery Company, 1962), p. 309. The original edition appeared in London in 1861.

9. Ibid., p. 314.

10. John Stuart Mill,*The Autobiography* (Garden City, New York: Doubleday and Company, no date), pp. 162-163. See particularly the statement "I contributed materially to this result", p. 163. See also *Considerations*, p. 338.

11. Mill, *Considerations*, p. 317.

12. Another distinguished liberal, Walter Bagehot, seems to have shared Mill's views on the limitations of a federal form of integration. However, in his case, there does appear to be a failure to grasp the distinctiveness of

a federal system when he insists on interpreting the breakup of American federalism by using the Hobbesian notion of sovereignty. This not only leads him to cede a good deal to the arguments of the Secessionists, but it indicates that he was not aware of the influence of Montesquieu's conception of political supremacy on the original Federalists. Or at least, he does not see that the conflict, on its ideological side, may well have centred on two incompatible conceptions of political supremacy. While the Montesquieu definition of supremacy is quite consistent with federal division of powers, the Hobbesian conception of sovereignty is not. See Walter Bagehot, *The English Constitution* (London: Collins, 1963), pp. 214–216.

Our point is that there was little support for federalism within the most progressive element of British liberalism and that Canadian liberals were generally more conservative than the British reformers. In addition, of course, the crisis of American federalism left the supporters of Confederation without a positive model.

13. On this score, the testimony of Hector Langevin is noteworthy. In letters to his wife, he expressed his fear that Macdonald will not keep his word. He says that "supported particularly by the *Times* of London, he is doing an about face at the last minute. Relying on the centralizing tendencies of Lord Carnarvon and Lord Monck, he is trying everything to obtain a legislative union rather than a federal one". Andrée Désilets, *Hector-Louis Langevin, un père de la Confédération (1826–1906)*, (Québec: Les Presses de l'Université Laval, 1969), pp.164–165. Later, in triumph, he writes that he has succeeded in thwarting Macdonald's efforts, ibid., p. 165.

14. Arend Lijphart, "Consociational Democracy", in Kenneth D. McRae, ed., *Consociational Democracy: Political Accommodation in Segmented Societies* (Toronto: McClelland and Stewart, 1974), p.75.

15. For further discussion on this general area, see Bruce W. Hodgins, "Democracy and the Ontario Fathers of Confederation", in *Profiles of a Province: Studies in the History of Ontario* (Toronto: Ontario Historical Society, 1967), pp. 83–91.

16. Robert Kelley notes the agreement between John A. Macdonald and George Brown in opposition to universal suffrage. *The Transatlantic Persuasion, The Liberal Democratic Mind in the Age of Gladstone* (New York: Alfred A. Knopf, 1969), pp. 367–9.

17. C. B. Macpherson, *The Real World of Democracy* (Toronto: CBC, 1965), p. 6.

18. Since J. S. Mill is one of the few political theorists mentioned in the Confederation Debates, we assume some acquaintance with his positions on the part of the Debate participants. For the development of Mill's thought on democracy, see J. H. Burns, "J. S. Mill and Democracy, 1829–1861", J. B. Schneewind, ed., *Mill: A Collection of Critical Essays* (Garden City, New York: Doubleday and Company, 1958), pp. 280–328.

19. Mill, *Considerations*, p. 328.

20. Robert Kelley, *The Transatlantic Persuasion*, p. 367.

21. Hanna F. Pitkin, *The Concept of Representation* (Berkeley: University of California Press, 1967), Chapter 7, pp. 144–167. See for example the remarks of John A. Macdonald: "Sir, we in this House are representatives of the people, and not mere delegates; and to pass such a law would be robbing ourselves of the character of representatives". *Debates*, p. 1004.

22. Hanna F. Pitkin, ed., "Introduction", *Representation* (New York: Atherton Press, 1969), p. 21.

23. Ibid., p. 20. The author has discussed the theory at greater length in *The Concept of Representation*, Chapter 8 passim.

24. For example, see the remarks of Cartier, *Debates*, pp. 57–62; and Macdonald, pp. 27–28, pp. 31–32, and p. 43.

25. For Wise's position, see

"Conservatism and Political Development: The Canadian Case", *South Atlantic Quarterly*, Vol. LXIX, No. 2 (Spring 1970), pp. 226–243; and "Upper Canada and the Conservative Tradition", in *Profiles of a Province*, pp. 20–33.

26. The distinctions between these two ideological persuasions are covered in greater detail in W. L. White, R. H. Wagenberg, and R. C. Nelson, *Introduction to Canadian Politics and Government*, 2nd ed. (Toronto: Holt, Rinehart, and Winston, 1977). See Chapter 2, "Ideological Determinants".

27. Alan Bullock and Maurice Shock, eds., *The Liberal Tradition from Fox to Keynes* (New York: New York University Press, 1957), p. 56. That Macaulay was correct in his assertion about the misunderstanding of the non-intervention principle's application to public works or internal improvements can be verified by reference to the writings of Adam Smith in 1776, Thomas Malthus in 1820, J. B. Say in 1821, Nassau Senior in 1831, and Frédéric Bastiat in 1850. See D. P. O'Brien, *The Classical Economists* (Oxford: Clarendon Press, 1975).

28. Goldwin Smith, *Reminiscences* (New York: The Macmillan Company, 1910), p. 231. The case for or against public financing in this domain was also considered a matter of expediency and not of principle by two American proponents of non-intervention who addressed themselves to the issue in the first half of the nineteenth century. The politician Henry Clay, in a famous speech in 1818, stressed the circumstantial aspects of the problem of financing public works and maintained that in new countries, private capital accumulation would be insufficient to perform this function. Guy S. Callender, *Selections from the Economic History of the United States 1765–1860* (New York: A. M. Kelley, 1965), pp. 393–395. The economist Henry Vethake, writing in 1844, re-examined the issue and

argued as well that the solution was not to be decided by recourse to principle, but by weighing advantages and disadvantages of various alternatives. Vethake was particularly concerned about the establishment of a private monopoly, such as the kind which resulted later during the period of railway construction. Henry Vethake, *The Principles of Political Economy*, Reprints of Economic Classics (New York: A. M. Kelley, 1971), pp. 313–316.

29. Louis Hartz, *The Liberal Tradition in America* (New York: Harcourt, Brace and World, 1955).

30. Louis Hartz, *The Founding of New Societies* (New York: Harcourt, Brace and World, 1964).

31. Ibid., pp. 6–10.

32. Ibid., p. 10.

33. Kenneth D. McRae, "The Structure of Canadian History", in Hartz, *The Founding of New Societies*, pp. 219–220. For later views of McRae on the Hartz thesis see his paper, "Louis Hartz's Concept of the Fragment Society and Its Application to Canada", presented to the Colloquium on Ideology and Political Life jointly sponsored by L'association française d'études canadiennes and York University, Toronto, October, 1977.

34. Ibid., pp. 234–244.

35. Gad Horowitz, "Conservatism, Liberalism, and Socialism in Canada: An Interpretation", *Canadian Journal of Economics and Political Science*, Vol. XXXII (May 1966), pp. 148–152. For Horowitz' reply to various critics, see "Notes on 'Conservatism, Liberalism, and Socialism in Canada'", *Canadian Journal of Political Science*, Vol. XI (June 1978), pp. 383–399.

36. Ibid., pp. 153–154.

37. "Perhaps never in French Canada were ideological differences expressed as directly as they were in the debates and political alignments between 1850 and 1860" Bernard, *Les Rouges*, p. 5.

38. Hartz, *The Founding of New Societies*, p. 14.

39. For additional evidence on the same

point see J. M. S. Careless, "Mid-Victorian Liberalism in Central Canadian Newspapers, 1850–1867", *Canadian Historical Review*, Vol. XXXI (Sept. 1950), pp. 233–236.

40. Seymour Martin Lipset, *Revolution and Counterrevolution: Change and Persistence in Social Structures*, rev. ed. (Garden City; Doubleday and Co., 1970), pp. 55–62.

41. Ibid., pp. 37–39. We must point out that in recent writings Lipset has re-evaluated his earlier positions, placing greater emphasis on structural variables in explaining Canadian-American differences. See his "Radicalism in North America: A Comparison of Views of the Party Systems in Canada and the United States", *Transactions of the Royal Society of Canada*, Series IV, Vol. XIV (1976), pp. 19–55.

42. Ibid., pp. 55–75.

43. Robert M. Calhoon, *The Loyalists in Revolutionary America, 1760-1781* (New York: Harcourt, Brace, Jovanovich, 1973), p. 504. David V. J. Bell has dealt with consequences of the Loyalist migration to Canada in "The Loyalist Tradition in Canada", *Journal of Canadian Studies*, Vol. V (May 1970), pp. 22–23.

44. To the extent that the Lower Canadian Conservatives shared the attitudes of the Ultramontane ideology of ecclesiastical leaders like Monsignors Lartigue and Bourget, they can be affiliated with the counterrevolutionary current widespread in France and associated with the names of De Bonald and De Maistre. Fernand Ouellet describes the second half of the nineteenth century in Lower Canada as "the golden age of the influence of Veuillot, De Bonald, and De Maistre and of all the more or less talented theocrats". "Nationalisme et Laicisme au XIXe siecle", Jean-Paul Bernard, *Les idéologies québeçoises au 19e siècle* (Montreal: Les Editions du Boréal Express, 1973), p. 55. See also p. 41 and p. 53. For a not unsympathetic look at the ideas of De Bonald and De Maistre see Thomas Molnar, *The Counter-*

Revolution (New York: Funk and Wagnalls, 1969).

45. All the indications are that 1858 marked the high point of Rouge influence in Canadian politics, the politics of the Union. Bernard, *Les Rouges*, p. 192. This was also the year in which Monsignor Bourget began his barrage of pastoral letters aimed at the Institut Canadien and liberalism generally. Philippe Sylvain, "Quelques aspects de l'antagonisme liberal-ultramontane au Canada français", Jean-Paul Bernard, *Les idéologies québeçoises*, p. 138.

46. The view that public expenditure for internal improvements was not incompatible with liberalism was stated by Thomas B. Macaulay in a speech to the House of Commons in 1846. Macaulay said that it was a misunderstanding of the principle of non-interference which prevented those who should act on behalf of the nation from supporting public transportation. "Consequently, numerous questions which were really public,/and he is referring specifically to the railway/questions which concerned the public convenience, the public property, the public security, were treated as private questions. That the whole society was interested in having a good system of internal communications seemed to be forgotten." Alan Bullock and Maurice Shock, eds., *The Liberal Tradition from Fox to Keynes* (New York: New York University Press, 1957), p. 56.

47. The senate was indeed seen as exercising a supervisory role over the House. John A. Macdonald called the Senate "a regulating body calmly considering the legislation initiated by the popular branch, and preventing any hasty or ill considered legislation which may come from that body . . . ". J. A. Macdonald, in *Parliamentary Debates on the Subject of the Confederation of the British North American Provinces* (Quebec: Hunter and Rose and Co., 1865), p. 36. The sentiment is that of Disraeli's

protagonist Coningsby who asks Mr. Millbank at the time of the Reform Bill of the 1830s, "Is not the revising wisdom of a senate a salutary check on the precipitation of a popular assembly?". Benjamin Disraeli, *Coningsby, or the New Generation* (New York: Capricorn, 1961; original 1846), pp. 207–8. It may be noted that Mr. Millbank was not convinced that popular assemblies tended to be precipitate, nor did he think the senate (House of Lords) would be strong enough to restrain the assembly (House of Commons).

48. For additional evidence questioning Lipset's assertions regarding Canadian conservatism see Tom Truman, "A Critique of Seymour M. Lipset's Article, 'Value Differences, Absolute or Relative: The English-Speaking Democracies'", *Canadian Journal of Political Science*, Vol. IV (December 1971), pp. 497–525.

49. Arend Lijphart, "Consociational Democracy", in Kenneth D. McRae, ed., *Consociational Democracy: Political Accommodation in Segmented Societies* (Toronto: McClelland and Stewart, 1974), p. 75.

50. Ibid., p. 82.

51. Arend Lijphart, "Cultural Diversity and Theories of Political Integration", *Canadian Journal of Political Science*, Vol. IV (March 1971), pp. 1–14.

52. S. J. R. Noel, "Consociational Democracy and Canadian Federalism", in McRae, ed., *Consociational Democracy*, pp. 264–265.

53. Robert Presthus, *Elite Accommodation in Canadian Politics* (Toronto: Macmillan of Canada, 1973), pp. 8–9.

54. Ibid., p. 9.

55. Ibid., pp. 9–10.

56. Kenneth McRae, "Epilogue", in McRae, ed., *Consociational Democracy*, p. 300.

57. Kenneth D. McRae, "Consociationalism and the Canadian Political System", in ibid., pp. 255–256.

58. Ibid., p. 256.

59. Arend Lijphart, *Democracy in Plural Societies: A Comparative Exploration*

(New Haven: Yale University Press, 1977), pp. 119–129.

60. Ibid., p. 127.

61. Ibid., pp. 124–127.

62. See especially Brian Barry, "The Consociational Model and Its Dangers", *European Journal of Political Research* Vol. IV (December 1975), pp. 398–399; and Steven B. Wolinetz, "The Politics of Non-Accommodation in Canada: Misapplications of Consociational Models and Their Consequences for the Study of National Integration and Political Stability", paper prepared for presentation to the Annual Meeting of the Canadian Political Science Association, London, Ontario, May, 1978.

63. See above, Chapter 5.

64. See above, Chapter 5.

65. See above, Chapter 5. See also, George F. G. Stanley, "The Federal Bargain: The Contractarian Basis of Confederation", in McRae, ed., *Consociational Democracy*, pp. 278–280.

66. The young Cartier was described as "one of the most fervent disciples of Papineau" and an active participant in the Rebellion of 1837. John Boyd, *Sir George Etienne Cartier* (Toronto: Macmillan Co. of Canada, 1914), p. 46. On his return from exile, his reflections on politics led him to work within the new system of responsible government and to eschew radicalism. In 1848 when the Lower Canadian Liberals split, Cartier followed the Lafontaine wing (right), rather than the Dorion wing (left), which was later to fuse with the Conservatives. Thus Cartier made the journey from being a Son of Freedom to being a stalwart Tory. On his relation with Lafontaine, see Alfred D. De Celles, *Cartier et son temps*, (Montreal: Librairie Beauchemin, 1913) pp. 73 et seq.

67. See especially Cartier's comments, *Debates*, pp. 60–61.

68. Ibid, see the remarks of Perrault, pp. 613–614 and of Joly, pp. 357–358.

69. Ibid., see the remarks of M. C. Cameron, pp. 452 ff, and p. 717; Scatcherd, p. 759; and Holton p. 147 and pp. 706–707.

70. For a further discussion of the

concept of elite accommodation, see
S. J. R. Noel, "Political Parties and
Elite Accommodation:
Interpretations of Canadian
Federalism", in J. Peter Meekison,
ed., *Canadian Federalism: Myth or
Reality?*, 2nd ed. (Toronto:
Methuen, 1971), pp. 121–140.

71. Indeed, Professor Smiley has
indicated that the relations between
the members of the executive
branch, both bureaucrats and
cabinet ministers, which he calls
"executive federalism", is the most
important aspect of the
contemporary federal system.
Smiley, *Canada in Question*, pp. 54–
82.

72. Charles A. Beard, *An Economic
Interpretation of the Constitution of
the United States* (New York:
Macmillan, 1913).

73. For example, Douglas McCalla,
"Tom Naylor's *A History of
Canadian Business, 1967–1914:* A
Comment", *Canadian Historical
Association. Papers* (1976), p. 249.

74. W. A. Mackintosh, "Economic
Factors in Canadian History", in
Ramsay Cook, Craig Brown, and
Carl Berger, eds., *Approaches to
Canadian History* (Toronto:
University of Toronto Press, 1967),
p. 12.

75. Ibid., p. 11.

76. D. G. Creighton, "Economic
Nationalism and Confederation", in
Ramsay Cook, Craig Brown, and
Carl Berger, eds., *Confederation*
(Toronto: University of Toronto
Press, 1967), p. 1. In fairness to
Creighton, he points out that his
essay is not an "economic
interpretation" of Confederation.

77. Ibid., p. 7.

78. R. T. Naylor, "The Rise and Fall of
the Third Commercial Empire of the
St. Lawrence", in Gary Teeple, ed.,
*Capitalism and the National Question
in Canada* (Toronto: University of
Toronto Press, 1972), p. 15.

79. R. T. Naylor, *The History of
Canadian Business, 1867–1914*, 2
Vols. (Toronto: James Lorimer and
Company, 1975).

80. Naylor, "The Rise and Fall", pp. 17
–18.

81. Creighton, "Economic Nationalism",
pp. 7–8.

82. Naylor, "The Rise and Fall", p. 15.
Just as legitimate an interpretation
of George Brown's remarks
regarding the increases in the yield
of Canadian bonds, is that it would
make the attraction of capital for the
development of facilities making
industrial expansion all the more
possible. It is true that the railway
was envisioned by some as a means
of continuing to foster a mercantilist
system, but one is hard put to find
any argument that can deny that an
influx of capital for these purposes
would not also encourage the
manufacturing sector. See *Debates*,
pp. 98–99.

83. C. P. Stacey, "Britain's Withdrawal
from North America, 1864–1871",
Canadian Historical Review, Vol.
XXXVI (Sept. 1955), pp. 187–188. See
also, Chester Martin, "British Policy
in Canadian Confederation",
Canadian Historical Review, Vol. XII
(March 1932), pp. 3–19.

84. Reginald G. Trotter, "Some
American Influences Upon the
Canadian Federation Movement",
Canadian Historical Review, Vol. V
(Sept. 1924), p. 215.

85. Robin W. Winks, *Canada and the
United States: The Civil War Years*
(Baltimore: The Johns Hopkins
Press, 1960), p. 379.

86. *Debates*, pp. 32–33.

87. Ibid., p. 145.

88. Ibid., p. 85.

89. By theoretico-practical thinking we
mean theory related to practice, not
as pure theory is related to
application, but as directive
knowledge about action. Madison in
the 10th Federalist Paper provides
an example of this kind of thought.
He begins with a discussion of the
divisive effects of political faction in
terms of achieving the public good.
He admits the undesirable political
consequences of factions, but he also
sees that a consequence of
suppression would be the loss of
liberty. The problem, then, must be
understood in its roots. Factions are
based on property differences,
differences of economic interests.

These interests are traced back to
fundamental differences in human
nature. This analysis leads Madison
to say that since there are natural
differences underlying economic and
political differences, one should
attempt to control the effects of
factionalism in a republic, rather
than trying to suppress it. The
analysis (theoretical) is for the
purpose of dealing with a matter
requiring decision and action
(practical). Hence we refer to this
thinking as theoretico-practical.

90. In this sense we do not find the
liberal-conservative ideological split
described by S. F. Wise. See his
"Liberal Consensus or Ideological
Battleground: Some Reflections of
the Hartz Thesis", *Canadian
Historical Association Reports* (1974),
pp. 1–14.
91. J. M. S. Careless, "'Limited
Identities' in Canada", *Canadian
Historical Review*, Vol. L (March
1969), pp. 1–10.

Bibliography

Primary

Parliamentary Debates on the Subject of the Confederation of the British North American Provinces. Quebec: Hunter and Rose, 1865.

Secondary

SOURCE MATERIALS

Census of Canada 1870. Vols. I, II, Ottawa: I. B. Taylor, 1873.

HALPENNY, FRANCESS G. (ed.). *Dictionary of Canadian Biography*, Vol. IX. Toronto: University of Toronto Press, 1976.

JOHNSON, J. K. (ed.). *The Canadian Directory of Parliament*. Ottawa: Public Archives of Canada, 1968.

LA TERREUR, MARC (ed.). *Dictionary of Canadian Biography*, Vol. X. Toronto: University of Toronto Press, 1972.

MORGAN, HENRY J. (ed.). *The Canadian Parliamentary Companion*. Quebec: Desbarats & Derbishire, 1862–1873. (place of publication and publisher vary in later editions).

——— . *Sketches of Celebrated Canadians and Persons Connected with Canada*. Montreal: R. Worthington, 1865.

——— (ed.). *The Dominion Annual Register and Review*. Ottawa: Maclean, Roger & Co., 1880–1886. (place of publication and publisher vary in later editions).

ROSE, GEORGE M. *A Cyclopaedia of Canadian Biography*. Toronto: Rose Publishing Co., 1886.

WALLACE, W. STEWART (ed.). *The Macmillan Dictionary of Canadian Biography*. Toronto: Macmillan, 1955, 1963.

BOOKS

BAGEHOT, WALTER. *The English Constitution*. London: Collins, 1963.

BASTIAT, FREDERIC. *Economic Harmonies*. Princeton: Van Nostrand, 1964.

BEARD, CHARLES A. *An Economic Interpretation of the Constitution of the United States.* New York: Macmillan, 1913.

BERNARD, JEAN-PAUL. *Les Rouges: Libéralisme, Nationalisme et Anti-cléricalisme au milieu du XIXe siècle.* Montreal: Les Presses de l'université du Québec, 1971.

BERNARD, JEAN-PAUL. *Les idéologies québecoises au 19e siècle.* Montreal: Les Editions du Boréal Express, 1973.

BLACK, E. R. *Divided Loyalties: Canadian Concepts of Federalism.* Montreal: McGill-Queen's Press, 1975.

BOWLEY, MARIAN. *Nassau Senior and Classical Economics.* London: G. Allen and Unwin, 1937.

BOYD, JOHN. *Sir George Etienne Cartier.* Toronto: Macmillan Co. of Canada, 1914.

BULLOCK, ALAN and MAURICE SHOCK (eds.). *The Liberal Tradition from Fox to Keynes.* New York: New York University Press, 1957.

CALHOON, ROBERT M. *The Loyalists in Revolutionary America, 1780–1781.* New York: Harcourt, Brace, Jovanovich, 1973.

CALLENDER, GUY S. *Selections from the Economic History of the United States, 1765–1860.* New York: A. M. Kelley, 1965.

CARELESS, J. M. S. *Brown of the Globe,* Vol. I, *The Voice of Upper Canada 1818–1859.* Toronto: Macmillan, 1959; Vol. II, *Statesman of Confederation, 1860–1880.* Toronto: Macmillan, 1963.

―――. *The Union of the Canadas: The Growth of Canadian Institutions, 1841–1857.* Toronto: McClelland and Stewart, 1967.

CHRISTIAN, W. and C. CAMPBELL. *Political Parties and Ideologies in Canada.* Toronto: McGraw-Hill Ryerson, 1974.

COOK, RAMSAY, JOHN C. RICKER, and JOHN T. SAYWELL. *Canada, A Modern Study.* Toronto: Clarke, Irwin and Co., 1967.

COOK, RAMSAY. *Canada and the French-Canadian Question.* Toronto: Macmillan, 1966.

COOK, RAMSAY, CRAIG BROWN, and CARL BERGER (eds.). *Approaches to Canadian History.* Toronto: University of Toronto Press, 1967.

COOK, RAMSAY, CRAIG BROWN, and CARL BERGER (eds.). *Confederation* Toronto: University of Toronto Press, 1967.

CORNELL, PAUL G. *The Alignment of Political Groups in Canada: 1841–1867.* Toronto: University of Toronto Press, 1962.

CREIGHTON, DONALD G. *Dominion of the North.* Toronto: Macmillan, 1962.

―――. *The Commercial Empire of the St. Lawrence 1760–1850.* Toronto: Ryerson Press, 1937.

―――. *The Road to Confederation: The Emergence of Canada 1863–1867.* Toronto: Macmillan, 1964.

────── . *John A. Macdonald*, Vol. I, *The Young Politician*. Toronto: Macmillan, 1952; Vol. II, *The Old Chieftain*. Toronto: Macmillan, 1955.

CURRIE, A. W. *Canadian Economic Development*, rev. ed. Toronto: Thomas Nelson and Sons, 1951.

DAWSON, R. MACGREGOR. *The Government of Canada, 4th ed.*, rev. by Norman Ward. Toronto: University of Toronto Press, 1963.

DAWSON, RICHARD E. and KENNETH PREWITT, *Political Socialization*. Boston: Little Brown, 1969.

DE CELLES, ALFRED D. *Cartier et son temps*. Montreal: Librairie Beauchemin, 1913.

DE JOUVENAL, BERTRAND. *The Pure Theory of Politics*. New Haven: Yale University Press, 1963.

DENNIS, JACK. *Socialization to Politics*. New York: John Wiley, 1971.

DENT, J. C. (ed.). *Canadian Portrait Gallery*. 4 Vols. Toronto: J. B. Maguin, 1880–1881.

DESILETS, ANDREE. *Hector-Louis Langevin: un père de la Confédération Canadienne 1826–1906*. Quebec: Les Presses de L'Université Laval, 1969.

DE TOQUEVILLE, ALEXIS. *Journey to America*. New Haven: Yale University Press, 1959.

DISRAELI, BENJAMIN. *Coningsby, or the New Generation*. New York: Capricorn, 1961.

DUCHACEK, IVO D. *Comparative Federalism: The Territorial Dimension in Politics*. New York: Holt, Rinehart, and Winston, 1970.

DUMONT, FERNAND. *La Vigile du Québec*. Montreal: Hurtubise, 1971.

DURHAM, J. C. L. *The Report of the Earl of Durham*. London: Methuen, 1905.

DRESCHER, SEYMOUR. *Tocqueville and England*. Cambridge: Harvard University Press, 1964.

EASTERBROOK, W. T. and M. A. WATKINS (eds.). *Approaches to Canadian Economic History*. Toronto: McClelland and Stewart, 1967.

EASTON, DAVID and JACK DENNIS. *Children in the Political System*. New York: McGraw-Hill, 1969.

ENGLEMANN, F. C. and M. A. SCHWARTZ. *Political Parties and the Canadian Social Structure*. Scarborough: Prentice-Hall, 1967.

FRIEDRICH, CARL J. *Trends of Federalism in Theory and Practice*. New York: Frederick A. Praeger, 1968.

GROULX, LIONEL. *La Confédération Canadienne*. Montreal: Le Devoir, 1913.

HAMMOND, M. O. *Confederation and its Leaders*. New York: George H. Doran, 1917.

HARRIS, R. COLE and JOHN WARKENTIN. *Canada Before Confederation: A Study in Historical Geography*. New York: Oxford University Press, 1974.

HARTZ, LOUIS. *The Founding of New Societies: Studies in the History of the United States, Latin America, South Africa, Canada, and Australia*. New York: Harcourt, Brace and World, 1964.

———. *The Liberal Tradition in America*. New York: Harcourt, Brace and World, 1955.

HESS, ROBERT D. and JUDITH V. TORNEY. *The Development of Political Attitudes in Children*. Chicago: Aldine, 1967.

HODGINS, BRUCE W. *John Sandfield Macdonald*. Toronto: University of Toronto Press, 1971.

HOLSTI, OLE R. *Content Analysis for the Social Sciences and Humanities*. Don Mills: Addison-Wesley, 1969.

HORN, MICHIEL and RONALD SABOURIN (eds.). *Studies in Canadian Social History*. Toronto: McClelland and Stewart, 1974.

JOHNSON, LEO A. *History of the County of Ontario, 1615–1875*. Whitby, Ontario: The Corporation of the County of Ontario, 1973.

KELLY, ROBERT. *The Transatlantic Persuasion: The Liberal Mind in the Age of Gladstone*. New York: Alfred A. Knopf, 1948.

KRUHLAK, O. M., R. SCHULTZ and S. J. POBIHUSHCHY (eds.). *The Canadian Political Process: A Reader*. Toronto: Holt, Rinehart, and Winston, 1973.

LIJPHART, AREND. *Democracy in Plural Societies: A Comparative Exploration*. New Haven: Yale University Press, 1977.

LIPSET, SEYMOUR MARTIN. *Political Man: The Social Bases of Politics*. Garden City: Doubleday and Company, 1966.

———. *Revolution and Counter-revolution: Change and Persistence in Social Structures*, rev. ed. Garden City: Doubleday and Company, 1970.

———. *The First New Nation*. Garden City: Doubleday and Company, 1967.

MAC DONALD, HELEN G. *Canadian Public Opinion on the American Civil War*. New York: Columbia University Press, 1926.

MACPHERSON, C. B. *The Real World of Democracy*. Toronto: CBC, 1965.

MALTHUS, THOMAS. *Principles of political economy considered with a view to their practical application*. New York: A. M. Kelley, 1951.

MALLORY, J. S. *The Structure of Canadian Government*. Toronto: Macmillan, 1971.

MARTIN, GED. *The Durham Report and British Policy*. Cambridge: Cambridge University Press, 1972.

MATTHEWS, DONALD R. *The Social Background of Political Decision-makers.* New York: Random House, 1954.

MC RAE, KENNETH (ed.). *Consociational Democracy: Political Accommodation in Segmented Societies.* Toronto: McClelland and Stewart, 1974.

MEEKISON, J. PETER (ed.). *Canadian Federalism: Myth or Reality?* 1st ed. Toronto: Methuen, 1968; 2nd ed., 1971.

MILL, JOHN STUART. *Considerations on Representative Government.* Chicago: Henry Regnery, 1962.

——. *The Autobiography.* Garden City: Doubleday, n.d.

MOLNAR, THOMAS. *The Counter-Revolution.* New York: Funk and Wagnalls, 1969.

MOORE, BARRINGTON JR. *Social Origins of Dictatorship and Democracy: Lord and Peasant in the Making of the Modern World.* Boston: Beacon Press, 1966.

MORTON, W. L. *The Critical Years: The Union of British North America, 1857–1873.* Toronto: McClelland and Stewart, 1964.

NAYLOR, R. T. *The History of Canadian Business, 1867–1914.* 2 Vols. Toronto: James Lorimer and Co., 1975.

NEW, CHESTER. *Lord Durham.* London: Dawsons of Pall Mall, 1968.

Ontario Historical Society (ed.). *Profiles of a Province: Studies in the history of Ontario.* Toronto: Ontario Historical Society, 1967.

ORMSBY, WILLIAM. *The Emergence of the Federal Concept in Canada, 1839–1845.* Toronto: University of Toronto Press, 1969.

OUELLET, FERNAND. *Histoire économique et sociale du Québec.* Montreal: Fides, 1966.

——. *Les Bas Canada 1791–1840: Changements structuraux et crise.* Ottawa: Editions de l'Université d'Ottawa, 1976.

PITKIN, HANNA F. *The Concept of Representation.* Berkely: University of California Press, 1967.

—— (ed.). *Representation.* New York: Atherton Press, 1969.

PRESTHUS, ROBERT. *Elite Accommodation in Canadian Politics.* Toronto: Macmillan of Canada, 1973.

RIKER, WILLIAM. *Federalism: Origin, Operation, Significance.* Boston: Little, Brown, 1964.

RUMILLY, ROBERT. *Histoire de la Province de Québec,* Vol. I. Montreal: Editions Bernard Valiquette, 1940.

SAY, J. B. *A Treatise on Political Economy.* New York: A. M. Kelley, 1964.

SCHNEEWIND, J. B. (ed.). *Mill: A Collection of Critical Essays.* Garden City: Doubleday, 1958.

SIMEON, RICHARD. *Federal Provincial Diplomacy: The Making of Re-*

cent Policy in Canada. Toronto: University of Toronto Press, 1972.

SKELTON, O. D. *The Life and Times of Sir Alexander Tilloch Galt.* Toronto: University of Toronto Press, 1920.

SKELTON, ISABEL. *The Life and Times of Thomas D'Arcy McGee.* Gardenvale: Garden City Press, 1925.

SMILEY, D. V. *Canada in Question: Federalism in the Seventies.* 2nd ed. Toronto: McGraw-Hill Ryerson, 1976.

——— (ed.) *The Rowell-Sirois Report: Book I.* Toronto: McClelland and Stewart, 1964.

SMITH, ADAM. *An Inquiry into the Nature and Causes of the Wealth of Nations.* New York: The Modern Library, 1937.

SMITH, GOLDWIN. *Reminiscences.* New York: The Macmillan Co., 1910.

STRAUSS, LEO. *Liberalism, Ancient and Modern.* New York: Basic Books, 1968.

TEEPLE, GARY (ed.). *Capitalism and the National Question in Canada.* Toronto: University of Toronto Press, 1972.

THOMSON, DALE C. *Alexander Mackenzie, Clear Grit.* Toronto: Macmillan, 1960.

THOMSON, D. C. and R. F. SWANSON. *Canadian Foreign Policy: Options and Perspectives.* Toronto: McGraw-Hill Ryerson, 1971.

THORBURN, HUGH G. (ed.). *Party Politics in Canada.* 2nd ed. Scarborough: Prentice-Hall, 1967.

UNDERHILL, FRANK H. *The Image of Confederation.* Toronto: Hunter Rose and Co., 1974.

——— . *In Search of Canadian Liberalism.* Toronto: Macmillan, 1960.

VETHAKE, HENRY. *The Principles of Political Economy.* New York: A. M. Kelley, 1971.

WADE, MASON. (ed.). *Canadian Dualism/La Dualité Canadienne.* Toronto: University of Toronto Press; and Laval: Presses Universitaires, 1960.

WAITE, P. B. *Confederation, 1854–1867.* Toronto: Holt, Rinehart, and Winston, 1972.

——— . *The Life and Times of Confederation 1864–1867: Politics, Newspapers and the Union of British North America.* Toronto: University Toronto Press, 1962.

WATTS, R. L. *New Federations: Experiments in the Commonwealth.* Oxford: Clarendon Press, 1966.

WHEARE, K. C. *Federal Government.* London: Oxford University Press, 1953.

WHITE, W. L., R. H. WAGENBERG, and R. C. NELSON. *Introduction to Cana-*

dian Politics and Government. 2nd ed. Toronto: Holt, Rinehart, and Winston, 1977.

WHITELAW, WILLIAM M. *The Maritimes and Canada before Confederation*. Toronto: Oxford University Press, 1934.

——. *The Quebec Conference*. Ottawa: The Canadian Historical Association Booklets No. 20, 1966.

WINKS, ROBIN W. *Canada and the United States: The Civil War Years*. Baltimore: John Hopkins Press, 1971.

WISE, S. F. and ROBERT CRAIG BROWN. *Canada Views the United States: Nineteenth Century Political Attitudes*. Toronto: Macmillan, 1967.

ARTICLES

BARRY, BRIAN. "The Consociational Model and Its Dangers". *European Journal of Political Research*, III (December 1975), 393–412.

BELL, DAVID V. J. "The Loyalist Tradition in Canada". *Journal of Canadian Studies*, V (May 1970), 22–33.

BLACK, E. R. "Federal Strains within a Canadian Party". *The Dalhousie Review*, XLV (Fall 1965), 307–323.

BRECHER, MICHAEL, BLEMA STEINBERG and JANICE STEIN. "A Framework for Research on Foreign Policy Behaviour." *Journal of Conflict Resolution*, XIII (March 1969), 75–101.

BROWN, G. W. "The Grit Party and the Great Reform Convention of 1859." *Canadian Historical Review*, XVI (September 1935), 245–265.

CAIRNS, ALAN C. "Alternative Styles in the Study of Canadian Politics." *Canadian Journal of Political Science*, VII (March 1974), 101–128.

——. "The Electoral System and the Party System in Canada." *Canadian Journal of Political Science*, I (March 1968), 55–80.

CARELESS, J. M. S. "'Limited Identities' in Canada." *Canadian Historical Review*, L (March 1969), 1–10.

——. "Mid-Victorian Liberalism in Central Canadian Newspapers 1850–1867". *Canadian Historical Review*, XXXI (September 1950), 221–236.

——. "The Toronto Globe and Agrarian Radicalism, 1850-67." *Canadian Historical Review*, XXIX (March 1948), 14–39.

CREIGHTON, D. G. "The United States and Canadian Confederation." *Canadian Historical Review*, XXXIX (September 1958), 209–222.

DOUGHTY, A. G. "The Awakening of Canadian Interest in the Northwest." *Canadian Historical Association Report* (1928), 5–11.

EASTON, DAVID and ROBERT HESS. "The Child's Political World." *Midwest Journal of Political Science*, VI (August 1962), 229–246.

EDINGER, LEWIS J. and DONALD D. SEARING. "Social Background in Elite Analysis: A Methodological Inquiry." *American Political Science Review*, LXI (June 1967), 428–445.

EDINGTON, ROBERT V. "The Ancient Idea of Founding and the Contemporary Study of Political Change". *Polity*, VII (Winter 1974), 163–179.

GEORGE, ALEXANDER. "'The Operational Code' Approach to the Study of Political Leaders and Decision-making". *International Studies Quarterly*, XIII (June 1969), 190–222.

HOLSTI, OLE. "The 'Operational Code' Approach to the Study of Political Leaders: John Foster Dulles' Philosophical and Instrumental Beliefs". *Canadian Journal of Political Science*, III (March 1970), 123–157.

HOROWITZ, GAD. "Conservatism, Liberalism, and Socialism in Canada: An Interpretation". *Canadian Journal of Economics and Political Science*, XXXII (May 1966), 143–171.

_____. "Notes on 'Conservatism, Liberalism, and Socialism in Canada'". *Canadian Journal of Political Science*, XI (June 1978), 383–399.

LANDON, FRED. "Canadian Opinion of Southern Secession, 1860–61". *Canadian Historical Review*, I (September 1920), 255–266.

LIJPHART, AREND. "Consociational Democracy". *World Politics*, XXI (January 1969), 207–225.

_____. "Cultural Diversity and Theories of Political Integration". *Canadian Journal of Political Science*, IV (March 1971), 1–14.

LIPSET, SEYMOUR MARTIN. "Radicalism in North America: A Comparison of Views of the Party Systems in Canada and the United States". *Transactions of the Royal Society of Canada*, Series 4, XIV (1976), 19–55.

MARTIN, CHESTER. "British Policy in Canadian Confederation". *Canadian Historical Review*, XII (March, 1932), 3–19.

Mc CALLA, DOUGLAS. "Tom Naylor's *A History of Canadian Business*, 1867–1914: A Comment". *Canadian Historical Association. Papers* (1976).

Mc LELLAN, DAVID S. "The 'Operational Code' Approach to the Study of Political Leaders: Dean Acheson's Philosophical and Instrumental Beliefs". *Canadian Journal of Political Science*, IV (March 1971), 52–75.

NOEL, S. J. R. "Consociational Democracy and Canadian Federalism". *Canadian Journal of Political Science*, IV (March 1971), 15–18.

SEARING, DONALD D. "The Comparative Study of Elite Socialization". *Comparative Political Studies*, I (January 1969), 471–500.

SPROUT, HAROLD and MARGARET. "Environmental Factors in the Study of International Politics". *Journal of Conflict Resolutions*, I (December 1957), 309–328.

STACEY, C. P. "Britain's Withdrawal from North America, 1864–1871". *Canadian Historical Review*, XXXVI (September 1955), 185–198.

——. "Fenianism and the Rise of National Feeling in Canada at the time of Confederation". *Canadian Historical Review*, XII (September 1931), 233–261.

STANLEY, G. F. G. "Act or Pact? Another look at Confederation". *Canadian Historical Association. Report* (1956), 1–25.

TROTTER, REGINALD G. "Some American Influences upon the Canadian Federation Movement". *Canadian Historical Review*, V (September 1924), 213–227.

TRUMAN, TOM. "A Critique of Seymour M. Lipset's Article, 'Value Differences, Absolute or Relative: The English-Speaking Democracies'". *Canadian Journal of Political Science*, IV (December 1971), 497–525.

UNDERHILL, FRANK H. "Some Aspects of Upper Canadian Radical Opinion in the Decade Before Confederation". *Canadian Historical Association. Report* (1927), 46–61.

WISE, S. F. "Conservatism and Political Development: The Canadian Case". *South Atlantic Quarterly*, LXIX (Spring 1970), 226–243.

——. "Liberal Consensus or Ideological Battleground: Some Reflections on the Hartz Thesis". *Canadian Historical Association. Report* (1974), 1–14.

PAPERS

BELL, DAVID V. J. "Methodological Problems in the Study of Canadian Political Culture". Paper presented at the 1974 meeting of the Canadian Political Science Association.

KEAR, A. R. "Confederalism: A New Theory of the Principles and Practices of Confederations". Paper presented at the 1976 meeting of the Canadian Political Science Association.

LAWRENCE, DONALD ARTHUR. "The 'Operational Code' of Lester B. Pearson". Paper presented at the 1974 meeting of the Canadian Political Science Association.

Mc RAE, KENNETH D. "Louis Hartz's Concept of the Fragment Society and Its Application to Canada". Paper presented to the Colloquium on Ideology and Political Life, jointly sponsored by L'Association française d'études canadiennes and York University. Toronto, October 1977.

WOLINETZ, STEVEN B. "The Politics of Non-Accommodation in Canada: Misapplications of Consociational Models and Their Consequences for the Study of National Integration and Political Stability". Paper presented at the 1978 meeting of the Canadian Political Science Association.